ONCE UPON A TIME
IN
CANADA

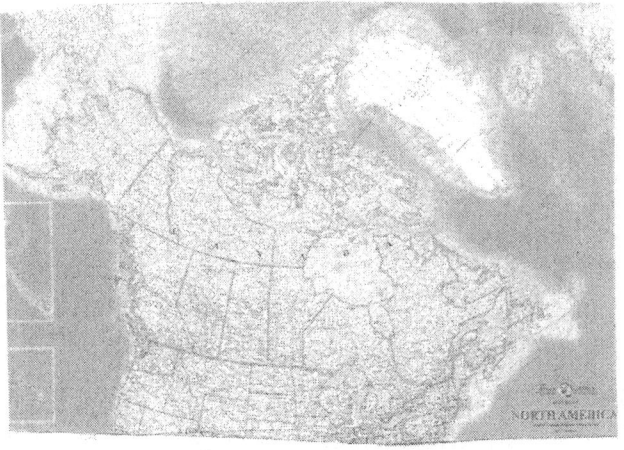

JOE REMESZ

ONCE UPON A TIME
IN
CANADA

JOE REMESZ

This is a work of historical fiction. All of the characters, organizations and events are products of the author's imagination or used fictitiously.

PROLOGUE

Quebec City, Canada – September 7, 1891

Wasyl Elaniak and Ivan Pylypiw stepped of the steamship Oregon in Quebec City as part of the mass immigration of Ukrainians to populate western Canada. They came to inspect the new lands about which they had heard so many favourable rumors and were pleased to discover that Canada had no peasants or gentry and all men were equal. They also discovered that a quarter section of land could be had for the unbelievably low price of $10.00. Elaniak and Pylpiw felt like they had hit the jackpot.

Ivan returned to Ukraine to get their families in the village of Nebyliw in the Kahush district while Wasyl remained in Canada to work. The Ukrainian government wasn't pleased with the exodus and with Ivan's return, so he was thrown in jail for "Agitating" the villagers to immigrate to Canada. In 1892, while Ivan was in jail, a group consisting of family and friends made the trip to Canada.

They settled in Edna, later renamed Star, Northwest Territories (Alberta) near Edmonton, which became the first Ukrainian settlement in Canada. Negative propaganda about Canada, spread by the landlords, put a damper on thoughts of emigration and only a trickle of Ukrainians came to Canada over the next several years. However, the problem which had led the Ukrainians to seek a new land to which they could emigrate remained. Soon another man took up their case.

In the summer of 1895, Dr. Josef Oleskiw, an agricultural professor born in the village of Nova Skvariava in Galicia, run by Poland and governed by the hostile Austro Hungarian Empire. (Now western Ukraine). Oleskiw promoted Ukrainian immigration to the Canadian prairie.

After hearing of the struggles of Ukrainian immigrants in Brazil, Oleskiw investigated alternative choices. He determined that the Canadian prairies were the most suitable for the Ukrainian farmers.
This lead to two pamphlets in Ukrainian – *About Free Land* and *On Emigration* and one in Polish *Vilni Zemli* in the spring of 1895. Oleskiw believed in selective immigration.

His first group of settlers were 30 handpicked families led by his brother, Vladimir, who arrived in Canada in Quebec City on April 30, 1896.

The majority of these immigrants settled in Edna, North West Territories (Now Alberta) and in Manitoba. They would encounter a problem, however: Would they be distinguished geopolitically or ethnically. Due to in part of the widespread distribution of Oleskiw's literature, Ukrainians became the largest Slavic group in Canada, with a population of 170,000 by 1914. Although Oleskiw promoted emigrants based on their assimilation tendencies, majority tended to retain their cultural heritage.

CHAPTER ONE

Lvov, Galicia, Poland – 1910

While having lunch, Pawlo Bilyi said to Petro Czorny, "Petro, as Ukrainians we hate the Poles as much as the Czechs hate the Hungarians and the Serbs, Austrians."
Petro set an Oleskiew pamphlet he was reading aside, and said, "You are right with that assessment. That is why we should move to Canada where we can enjoy freedom and free land."
Aware the Canadian government in conjunction with railway and steamship companies was making a concerted effort to colonize western Canada with central and eastern Europeans, the two university students were studying information the Canadian government and Dr. Oleskiw had distributed several years earlier.

Pawlo and Petro lived in Lvov, a city in the Austro-Hungarian Empire in the province of Galicia and run by Poland from 1772 to 1918. Here people spoke distinct languages besides numerous dialects.

There were Poles, Ruthenians's (also called Ukrainians and Rusyns in those days), Germans, Magyars, Italians, Turks, and Jews among others. It was a multinational land; well before anyone coined the term multiculturalism and for most part, they all coexisted in relative peace until Hitler and Stalin decided to redraw the map of Europe. It was a period when everyone paid allegiance to the Hapsburg monarch, the Austrian emperor, Franz Josef, who used ruthless measures to suppress the national yearnings of minorities. In Polish Galicia the ruthless measures were especially directed against those of Ruthenian heritage.

The conflict had reached a point where historians had ventured to prophesy that a General European war could probably end the ill-sorted conglomerate of Austro Hungarian states within several years.

It was a time in history when Russia concluded the war with Japan and the Industrial Revolution opened the way to Communism. Tsar Nicholas 11 continued his reaction policy.

For a moment it was thought the revolution had been stifled but in reality it had been drawn underground, and was destined to break forth with irresistible violence.

As for the Austria-Hungarian Empire, it had immediate dangers of its own which lay with the Croats and Serbs who inhabited the southern part of Galicia.

These people were closely related in their language, customs and traditions, both to each other and the Serbs who lived just beyond the frontiers, to the south.

The Serbs, Croats and Slovenes, thought of themselves as Southern Slavs and nurtured one common bond, an intense hatred for the Hungarians and Germans.

In the dimmed light of his parents' home, Petro had difficulty speaking because earlier in the day he and Pawlo were involved in a fist-fight between Polish and Ukrainian Lvov University students and received a terrible beating by the Polish students. Majority of the students were Poles but there were Ruthenians (Ukrainians) too.

Poles always frightened the Ruthenian students, including their leader Adam Kotosko, saying they were moscowphiles orientated towards Russia and, concerning ukrainianphiles, the difference was between Ruthenian and a Mscowphile was the same as the difference between a Jew and an Israelite. The students expressed their nationalism by the way they dressed, Poles in leather coats and four-cornered hats and Ruthenians in sheepskin coats, fur hats and leather boots. Poles emulated aristocracy and Ruthenians Cossack democracy, idealizing peasantry, and sometime vulgarity, to contrast with the pretentious manners of Poles.

"I wouldn't be surprised if the Polish students get back at Adam Kotosko, and beat him up one of these days," Petro said.

"You may be right. The fight the students on each side had was a traumatic experience and Kotosko was the instigator." Pawlo answered and picked up a booklet titled *About Immigration*. Dr. Oleskiw, a Ukrainian agriculturalist that had visited Canada earlier and assisted Ukrainians settling there. After reading several pages, Pawlo said, "Why don't you and I immigrate to Canada?

In his booklet Dr. Oleskiw says that Canada is the Promised Land, a better place to live in than for example, Brazil."

"But why is Canada a better place than Brazil?" Petro asked.

"Because slavery exists in Brazil and slave owners also use Ukrainian immigrants as cheap labor. As a matter of fact, Dr. Oleskiw says many Ukrainians are kept in slave lockups there."

Petro was twenty only a year older than Pawlo and both were tall, muscular, and blond and seemed older than their age.

Both dreamed passionately that someday they could lead independent lives and enjoy freedom, but since Poland was divided by the Austro-Hungarian and Russian empires, that possibility was unlikely so Petro said, "Okay. Why not? We will we escape compulsory military training in the Austrian army, poverty, shortage of land, heavy taxation, lack of freedom and unfavorable political conditions if we leave. We may also obtain opportunities in Canada that our parents never had."

Pawlo flipped through a write-up about Winnipeg in *About Immigration* and then picked up a brochure Petro had been studying published by the Canadian government extoling the virtues of western Canada explaining why one should emigrate there. The brochure was bylined by Clifford Sifton, Canada's minister of the Interior at the time. Under Sifton's name was the signature of Canada's Prime Minister, Wilfred Laurier.

"Who knows, you may even become the mayor of Winnipeg?" Petro teased.

"That would be all right," Pawlo answered.

"At the moment however, my dream is once we arrive in Canada, is to own a 160 acre homestead and eventually become an entrepreneur. What is your dream?"

Petro did not hesitate to answer, "My dream like, yours is to have freedom and make a fortune."

Besides obtaining a homestead, Pawlo and Petro were also determined to be entrepreneurs, but just how that would take place they, did not know.

They did know, however, that the death of Queen Victoria in Great Britain in 1901 had marked the close of an era and a change in the atmosphere.

There was an unceasing willingness to use force and violence to attain ends, as opposed to the old reliance of peaceful persuasion and debate.

It was a time in history when England and\Germany's economic rivalry paralleled their burgeoning arms race. It was a time Suffragettes as they had become known, began to force the government to acknowledge their demands, to turn to violence and even attack Buckingham Palace. The first decade of the 20th century saw prices rising faster than wages.

Labor anxious to close the gap between the two became more violent in its demands and this led to an epidemic of strikes.

Another difficulty was the most vexatious of British problems, the Irish Home Rule question.

The Liberals no longer had a clear majority in the House of Commons and were compelled to seek support of the eighty-six Irish Nationalist MP's in order to stay in power.

This support was sought at the price of passing the Third Home Rule. A complicating factor was that within Ireland, the province of Ulster, was utterly opposed to Home Rule, and did not hesitate to exploit English suspicions and misgivings to keep opposition burning at fever pitch.

Cork, Ireland – 1910

In southern Ireland, the city of Cork was falling into evening darkness as the Lee River flowed gently and the bells of Shandon in the tower of St. Anne's church rang out. Margaret and Erin Carpenter, petite, pretty and both twenty-one, were sitting in Margaret's typing room overlooking Tomas McCurtain's small clothing factory on Davis Street. The McCurtain's, like Margaret and Erin's parents, Sean and Anne Carpenter, had living quarters above their buildings. Both families were staunch Republicans. On this particular day Margaret and Erin were looking forward towards launching their careers as teachers in Canada.

"Next month we will be halfway across the Atlantic on our way to Winnipeg," Margaret said while picking up a copy of the Examiner newspaper.

The Carpenter twins were also thankful that their uncle, Henry Windsor, a Conservative member of the Canadian House of Commons, alerted his nieces of the need of teachers in Winnipeg and was paying their passage.

CHAPTER TW0

Winnipeg, Manitoba – 1910

Henry Windsor, next to Liberal MP Clifford Sifton, was probably the most important politician in Winnipeg. He had been born and raised in London where he had met his wife, Patricia. After Patricia gave up Roman Catholicism to become an Anglican, the couple immigrated to Canada in the mid 1880's. Now 35 years later, Windsor owned a chain of retail and wholesale stores which afforded him a prominent position in Winnipeg society. So did Windsor's twenty-three year-old son, John, who along with his father was also involved in speculative real estate.

It would be safe to say that on his arrival in Canada the senior Windsor became a nationalist and a xenophobe.

There were many times the senior Windsor argued with Sifton, the MP for Brandon, 175 miles west of Winnipeg, who was also owner and publisher of the *Winnipeg Free Press* newspaper.

One day during a debate in the House of Commons in Ottawa, Windsor pointed his finger at Sifton and angrily said, "Mr. Speaker. As Canada's former Minister of the Interior this honorable member made his greatest mistake when he let all those foreigners, the scum of Europe, into Canada."

The English in Winnipeg dominated the whole spectrum of human activity at the time, including: politics, business, the arts, education and the professions without exception. They were also active in farm organizations. Unions, Board of Trade, moral reform and social crusades, in all of these areas' the English held a monopoly.

Cork, Ireland – 1910

"Protestants and Catholics will soon have their own armies in Ireland. Who knows, with the bitterness which exists between the two groups, there could be fires, bombings and loss of lives." Erin said. Seeing her sister wasn't paying attention she went on, "Margaret, you aren't paying attention to what I'm saying."

In reply Margaret said, "I'm listening. It's just that I'm having difficulty in reading the newspaper. Look. It says a friend of yours, Jimmy McKernan, has been arrested by the Royal Irish Constabulary on instructions of the British government, and is to spend three months in Brixton prison in London."
Margaret rose from the typing table and walked towards the living room. On her way she passed the paper to Erin and said, "Here, your eye sight is better than mine. You can read the article yourself."
Erin admitted that she and Jimmy McKernan, a twenty-one year-old socialist had been involved in a scuffle about Home Rule with several Protestants. Being devout Catholics, Erin and Jimmy, were in favor of Home Rule. When Erin finished reading the article, she flipped through pages of the newspaper and came to a section marked 'today in History' which she read out loud.
"Seven years ago a group of Serbian officers, members of the secret nationalist organization called Black Hand, burst into the palace and murdered the Serbian King and Queen."
"There is no limit what people will do, even murder, when they are suppressed," Margaret who heard the reading, said.

Erin kept silent but when she finished reading the article, placed the newspaper to one side and went to the living room too where she approached Margaret and said, "I'm looking forward to living in Canada. We'll be sailing from Liverpool."

Lvov, Galicia, Poland – 1910

The decision for Pawlo and Petro to leave Poland wasn't an easy one and once made, the pair was beset with a variety of obstacles. They had to apply for identity papers and medical documents and arrange transportation to Liverpool."

Also their parents didn't want them to go and said that Canada was fraught with perils. Pawlo's mother warned, "A whale will jump on board the ship and in the mid-Atlantic and swallow both of you. And if it's not a whale that gets you, sharks will. And I'm not finished, there are huge icebergs off the coast of Canada that your ship may hit and you will drown."

To their credit, Pawlo and Petro, whose parents belonged to a relatively privileged class, were not afraid of the unknown.

They were young men ready to toil, to sweat, to sacrifice. They were going to leave Galicia with their faith, a faith that was to be tested. Fortunately they could speak English unlike most Ukrainians arriving in Canada.

"Someday you will come and visit us in Canada," Petro said to his mother whose health was failing.

Minutes later, she handed Petro a bag containing a mixture of pyerohy, holubtsi, poppy seed, bread and kolbasa and said, "Use the poppy seed in the bread you will bake to celebrate your success in Canada."

"At least the two of you won't have to serve in the Austrian army should there be a war." Pawlo's mother said as she handed her son a package.

"What's inside?" Pawlo asked to which his mother replied, "I prepared some food for you and Petro to enjoy while onboard ship."

"Thank you." Pawlo said and a minute later, his and Petro's parents began crying. Aside from the salty tears, their fear was that the money they had lent and the sons' themselves probably would never be seen again.

Casting a nostalgic glance at his beloved city of Lvov, Pawlo said to the parents," Don't worry, we will write and often."

Pawlo and Petro shook hands with their parents, waved 'Goodbye' and made their exit embarking on the long journey to the New World.

Liverpool, England – 1910

The two day journey meandered through Poland before reaching England. After reaching the port of Liverpool, Pawlo and Petro became disheartened because like all immigrants at the time in Europe, were harassed by hordes of pirates, swindlers selling counterfeit tickets and unscrupulous agents selling passage on ships that were barely seaworthy.

It was normal, just like in the rival port of Hamburg, Germany, for high-pressure jobbers to buttonhole immigrants and take them to disreputable inns or other places where they could be fleeced by lively assortment of thugs, thieves and prostitutes.

The port of Liverpool was crowded with people from many parts of Europe as Pawlo and Petro boarded the S. S. Christiana a 2811 tonne ship built in 1890.

Many passengers' carried with them only what was most precious to them: millstones, axe, sickle, linen, cutlery, or just clothing on their backs.

In some cases there were whole families of two and three generations leaving their relatives behind and spreading a branch of the family tree halfway around the world.

Leaving friends and relatives and ancestral villages was a traumatic experience.

On-board the ship, there were hundreds of men, women and children speaking many languages. Some did not designate themselves by name, Ukrainian, but by their origin as Austrian, Galician, Ruthenian, Bukovinian, Lemko, Hungarian or Russian, according to their place of birth as registered in their passports.

The two-week transatlantic voyage, like most voyages at the time, was the next ordeal for Pawlo and Petro. The ship was designed to carry cargo and passengers and there was little effort to adapt the ship for human comfort. Apart from bringing in provisions: flour, potatoes, oatmeal, tea, salted fish and water stored in rancid casks used previously for oil or other containments, the captain merely lay down a temporary deck over the cargo and constructed flimsy births that could be dismantled after the voyage.

Passengers were packed tightly; ventilation, sanitation and after a storm struck and waves began to splash against the ship, seasickness presented a serious problem.

As the ship kept crossing the Atlantic, Pawlo and Petro noticed two attractive women on the ship's deck who spoke only in English. As the ship sailed further and everyone overcame a period of sea sickness, Pawlo finally found enough courage to ask the young lady nearest to him, "Excuse me, madam, but to what part of Canada are you going?"

"Winnipeg," she replied. "And you?"

"We are going to Winnipeg too." Pawlo replied and then introduced himself and Petro. "My name is Pawlo Bilyi and this is my friend, Petro Czorny."

"I'm pleased to make your acquaintance. I'm Erin Carpenter and this is my twin sister, Margaret. We are from Cork, Ireland and will be teaching at a school in Winnipeg in September."

After shaking hands and exchanging pleasantries, Margaret turned to Petro and asked. "What country are you from?"

"We are Ukrainian living in the Austro-Hungarian province of Galicia in Poland." Petro replied and then the conversation switched to their background, trivial things and hobbies, which included playing cards. Erin also said that she enjoyed listening to music, and to dance.

Margaret said, "I enjoy writing and reading the words of James Joyce, George Bernard Shaw and William Butler Yeats and play the piano."

Both Petro and Pawlo, said they enjoyed working with the soil. Pawlo also said he was fond of reading and playing the violin. Both Pawlo and Petro said why they spoke English, although awkwardly, was because they had taken lessons from the clergy in Lvov whose name had changed many times. "It was even called Lemberg at one time," Pawlo said. "There are two classes of people in Lvow. Peasants who are simple and humble and theologians," Petro said in jest.

Once the formal introductions were made, the foursome became loquacious and friendly. They even played cards together. It was during a card game, that Margaret asked Petro what he thought of women who were demanding voting rights in England.

"I think it's a good idea. Mark my word; I wouldn't be surprised if England someday, had a woman prime minister."

It was the following day, Pawlo, Petro, Erin and Margaret met again, and since passengers had nothing to do, they began spending most of their time on the deck, talking to each other. That's when Pawlo said concerning the use of the English language, "Sorry. Sometimes we do not say things right but we learn quick."

"Quickly," Erin corrected Pawlo.

Petro then said, "I have pyrohy, holubtsi, bread and sausage that I want to share with you."

Erin and Margaret agreed to have lunch with the two young, handsome Ukrainian men.

After they had eaten, Margaret said, "Ten more days and we should arrive at the port of Quebec City."

What Erin said was, "I enjoyed the lunch. Thank you. The pyrohy and holubtsi were delicious."

The friendly relationship continued despite a storm when the ship reached mid-Atlantic and rain and hurricane-like winds tossed the ship from side to side.

 Passengers held on to the iron railings until the storm subsided and the ballast was returned to normal position.

Several days later, the foursome were playing cards again when a huge iceberg came into view, larger in size than the ship, as it floated majestically in the blue Atlantic Ocean. Pawlo recalled what his mother had said about icebergs and was sure there was a monster clinging to the ice but Margaret said there wasn't a thing on it, and told him where the icebergs came from, and where they went, and why the wind was so much colder than it had been.

CHAPTER THREE

Quebec City, Canada – 1910

When the S. S. Christiana docked in Quebec City, each immigrant had to pass through Customs and Immigration for identification. The immigration officer on duty at the time did not ask for a visa because one wasn't necessary. Instead he checked the passport and asked for Pawlo and Petro's name, age and destination. The officer then asked other questions one of which was, "And your nationality?"

"We are from Galicia," Pawlo replied.

The officer said in jest, "Did I hear you correctly; you say you are a Galilean, from Nazareth, perhaps?"

"Oh, no, I haven't been nailed to a cross yet, but my parents warned that I may as soon as I begin farming near Winnipeg. I'm from the province of Galicia that is part of the Austro-Hungarian Empire run by Poland." Pawlo said.

The officer making a note of the nationality as Austrian continued with the processing. "You are to have twenty-five dollars before you are permitted to land in Canada. Please, may I see your money?"

Pawlo and Petro became embarrassed. When they were counting their money, which had been sewn to their underwear for safety, they discovered they were each $5 short. They were short of funding, because they were fleeced in Liverpool when they had been led to believe their passage was subsidized. It turned out to be a lie on the steamship agent's part.

"If you can't come up with the other $5, I'm afraid you'll have to be deported back to Poland," the officer said.

Pawlo and Petro panicked and didn't know what to do. Fortunately Margaret overheard the conversation and lent each of the two young men the $5 required, so that they could remain in Canada.

The next step for each immigrant was to undergo a medical checkup, which Pawlo, Petro and Erin passed without difficulty but it wasn't for Margaret, because when the medical officer gave her a physical and came to her eyes, he said, "Miss Carpenter, I'm afraid we'll have to deport you back to Ireland."

Margaret knew that her vision wasn't the best, but deported back to Ireland seemed ludicrous and humiliation of the highest degree.

She became frightful and only Erin with the help of Pawlo and Petro calmed her down. "Deport me back to Ireland? Why?" she asked the medical officer.

"I don't make the rules here," the medical examiner replied. "You have a disease known as glaucoma that will eventually make you blind. Authorities feel blind people have little to contribute towards Canada's growth as a nation."

Margaret worried about of having to return to Ireland. She unburdened herself to the medical examiner by saying, "And if I had varicose veins, the same authorities would say that I should have my leg amputated?"

Margaret was surprised when the medical examiner said," We deported a woman with varicose veins last week."

Realizing the dilemma she was in, Margaret with the help of Erin used the latest communication technology and phoned her uncle, Henry Windsor, in Ottawa who at the time of the call, had just finished participating in a parliamentary debate in the House of Commons.

After hearing about the deportation threat, Windsor said, "Don't worry Margaret, I'll arrange for an eye specialist. What this needs is political clout.

You'll be on your way to Winnipeg as soon as I make several phone calls."
An hour later, Margaret, Erin, Pawlo and Petro were on their way to Winnipeg.

The coming of immigrants made for an exciting time to reach the Canadian Prairies. It was a time when Canadian trains were filled with Europeans traveling west in search of a better life and a homestead for ten dollars. These pioneer families, disembarking from railroad coaches, often traveled in ox-drawn wagons to their new homes through untamed forests or followed buffalo trails on the seemingly endless plains. The spirit of adventure was in the air and a great future beckoned one and all. European immigration into Canada was in full swing.

Ukrainian immigration was no different from other groups. They immigrated to escape war, famine, religious persecution, political persecution, freedom, seek a better life or the love of adventure to reach their goal. Immigrants faced many trials and tribulations.

The German and Ukrainian-speaking Mennonites led the way in 1874 by leaving the marshlands of southern Ukraine and settling in southern Manitoba and north-central Saskatchewan.

The Ukrainians from Galicia first arrived near Edmonton, Alberta in 1891, and then spread to southern Manitoba and across the parklands of central Saskatchewan.

Then from the Russian Empire came the Russian Doukhobors a Christian pacifist sect, from Siberia, in 1899 settling in Kamsack and Blaine Lake areas of Saskatchewan, with some later moving to the West Kootenay communities of Nelson, Castlegar and Grand Forks in southern British Columbia.

But now the sturdy peasants of the Steppes and Carpathian mountains in Ukraine, the Baltic lowlands of Poland and the Plains of Hungry were taming the Canadian prairie. Their passports showed only Austrian or Russian citizenship because Western Ukraine, Poland and Hungry were part of the Austro-Hungarian Empire, and Eastern Ukraine belonged to the Russian Empire.

The Ukrainian immigrants who came from the provinces of Galicia and Carpathian-Ukraine were eastern rite Greek Catholics, while those who originated from the Carpathian Mountains, and Eastern Ukraine, were Greek Orthodox. Both churches are of the Byzantine rite. Their religious tradition originated from the Greek Church in Constantinople, the capital city of the Eastern Roman Empire

Northern Ontario, Canada – 1910

The train journey from Quebec City to Winnipeg took another four days. The colonist train was primitive in nature. Coal burning stoves at each end of the cars provided the only heat. Dining facilities let much to be desired and most immigrants, like Pawlo and Petro, brought their own food The seats were made out of wood and a platform was located above the seats where a brave soul could climb up and attempt to sleep. Babies cried while the odor of dirty diapers and unwashed bodies permeated the cars.

As the train headed west, it passed through Montreal and towns and village with schools and churches with French signs on them. When the train reached northern Ontario, some passengers began to cry. They had never seen such a vast wilderness of muskeg, bush and rock. Some immigrants were even sorry that they had come to Canada.

Pawlo, Petro, Margaret and Erin, did not cry, they played cards. As they were playing a passenger approached Petro and speaking in half German and half English, said, "I want to tell you that I have watched you since we began our journey in Liverpool, but please tell me, why you aren't crying like everyone else?"

"Why cry?" Petro acknowledged the German, who identified himself as Hans Gruber.

"After seeing this wilderness some immigrants are saying it will be worse in Canada than living in Galicia."

"We have nothing to lose," Petro said and went on, "What could be worse than working for a Polish pahn."

"Oh yes, there is," Gruber said.

"What?"

"Some say working for an Englishman in Winnipeg."

What lay ahead? Had Pawlo Bilyi and Petro Czorny made a wrong decision? No time to think about it now. A new life and freedom was about to begin.

When Gruber returned to his seat, he stared out of the train's window, and said he felt abandoned by mankind and even God.

The following day, the barren Laurentian Shield, gave way to rich prairie farmland and those who cried earlier, including Gruber, felt greatly relieved.

As the train approached Winnipeg, Erin said to Pawlo while handing him a piece of paper, "Here is our address and phone number at our uncle's and aunt's residence."

"Do you want us to keep in touch?" Pawlo asked.

"Once you and Petro are settled, please do," and slipped a ten dollar bill in his hand, "Just in case," she said.

It was dark outside when the train pulled into Winnipeg and passengers disembarked. It was at this juncture that Erin introduced Pawlo and Petro to twenty three-year-old John Windsor who met the train.

The young Windsor then introduced his friend, a broad shouldered twenty four-year-old James Buller, to all of them.

CHAPTER FOUR

Winnipeg, Manitoba 1910

As soon as the introductions were completed, Pawlo and Petro walked to Immigration Hall where they would live for a while. John Windsor, James Buller and the Carpenter twins, meanwhile, drove in a Model T Ford to the Windsor residence in the south-end of Winnipeg, an exclusive neighborhood known for its affluence and inhabited by people of British origin.

This was a period in Canadian history when the country's population was seven-million, Winnipeg's 135.000, Calgary 46,000 and Edmonton 25,000. Automobiles were no longer a novelty in Winnipeg.

Durant's, Locomnobiles, Winton's, Columbia's, Model T Fords, Oldsmobile's and Buick's were already clogging the streets by those who were wealthy. As a matter of fact John Windsor was fined $10.00 for speeding his Motel T on Main Street the week before. He was clocked by police at seventeen miles an hour.

This was a time when Winnipeg could boast (and did) of having more millionaires to the acre than any other Canadian city. It had 19 compared to Toronto, which had 21. It was a time of knighthoods, when Winnipeg's leading businessmen were honored by the sovereign across the sea.

No city in North America had such absolute and complete command over the wholesale trade of the vast area. The city germinated from a hamlet of a few hundred people to being the third largest city in the Dominion with a population of just over 135,000.

In the city's Golden Age, the wealthy and the prominent would gather informally in the stately precincts of the Manitoba Club. It was above all, a grand time for the grain trade. Grain-merchant families all made their mark. Winnipeg, located in the centre of North America, was also one of the greatest commercial centres of the continent as it was a manufacturing community of great importance.

With the coming of the Canadian Pacific Railway in 1881 quiet little Winnipeg strode into adulthood.

The rails pushed ever westward to span Canada. Fattening on the rail building activity, Winnipeg almost overnight, became a boomtown dancing to the tune of popping champagne corks.

The new rails began to bring by the thousands the land-hungry immigrants from Europe – Ukrainians, Poles, Germans, Hungarians, Icelanders, Irish, Jews and others.

They came, they stayed, they continued further west to find newer provinces and cities, towns and villages. Breasting this human tide, Winnipeg was nicknamed the Chicago Of Canada and the corner of Portage and Main conjured images of biting winter winds, frostbite, blizzards, and policemen bundled in bulky buffalo-skin coats.

On the east side of the Red River, founded in 1818, stood St. Boniface, the largest French-speaking community west of the Great Lakes.

On arrival, Pawlo and Petro walked towards the centre of Winnipeg. Along the way they spotted a building with a sign APARTMENTS FOR RENT on it. When they enquired about accommodation Pawlo and Petro were surprised that the caretaker responsible for its operation was Ukrainian and came from Galicia as they did.

Nellie Kozak and the two new immigrants reminisced for an hour, talking about the Old Country, when Nellie said; "My husband, Nicholas, our son Metro and I arrived in Winnipeg on the same day that Queen Victoria died. Metro is a doctor now, but it wasn't easy for him to become one."

Petro, curious, said, "Why?"

"The reason is because the English don't want Slavs and Jews to be doctors in Winnipeg."

"Maybe Metro's marks weren't that good?"

"Oh, his marks were good, but Anglo Saxons try to exclude anyone that isn't one of them. I'm certain Metro will tell you all about it once you meet him."

Nellie said that her husband was employed by a draying company but not making much money.

"Why is that?" Petro asked. "According to brochures I have read, Canada is supposed to be a country of milk and honey."

"Milk and honey?" Nellie scoffed, "It's more like mustard and baloney. Nicholas puts in long hours working for a draying company, but the average wage for a ten-hour day is two dollars and fifty cents.

To meet ends meet and to pay off the bills, to educate Metro, and save a bit in case of an emergency, it is necessary to supplement our income by other means. That is why I'm a caretaker of this rooming house."

The room Pawlo and Petro chose was hot inside, there was no ventilation and the building itself appeared crowded with immigrants.

The two new tenants were comfortable, however, and the following day as they were shaving, looked out a window overlooking the city. What they saw was a large crowd gathering in front of City Hall.

"Why the large crowd? There must be one thousand people," Petro asked Nellie.

"The crowd is protesting the killing of Adam Kotosko in Lvov, during a fight between Polish and Ukrainian students."

A collection is being taken to help the Ukrainian students in the homeland to get even with the Poles. You can read about the explosive situation in tomorrow's edition of the *Ukrainian Voice* newspaper."

Next day, Pawlo and Petro not only read about Adam Kotesko's death, but also that Winnipeg was becoming highly concentrated with Ukrainian immigrants. They were the largest single ethnic group and along with other foreigners, including Jews, kept pouring in. At the invitation of the Canadian government 170, 000 Ukrainians came to Canada in the early 1900's to escape the Austria-Hungarian government. Majority were illiterate and without capital because of the "exorbitant prices" which these new immigrants were charged.

As a member of parliament, Henry Windsor had protested in the House of Commons frequently, but since he was an opposition member, nothing seemed to be done about it. Sifton, who resigned as Minister of the Interior in 1905, but still an active member for the Liberals, was indifferent each time Windsor complained.

On one occasion Prime Minister Laurier said, "I'm still of the opinion that a stalwart peasant in a sheepskin coat, born of soil, whose forefathers have been farmers for generations, with a stout wife and half a dozen children is a good quality.

These men are workers. They have been bred by generations to work from daylight to dark. They have never done anything else and never expect to do anything else."
Sifton was only partially correct. Many immigrants described as Pauper Immigrants did want to do something else if given the opportunity

Pawlo and Petro were single men, determined to work from daylight to darkness, but their wives would not be stout. Both had thoughts running through their minds that the wives they would choose would be lean and pretty, about twenty and Irish. It was July 1910.

CHAPTER FIVE

Winnipeg - 1910

It was in August when Dr. Metro Kozak invited Pawlo and Petro to his residence in the North-end of Winnipeg. After the doctor introduced the young men to his wife, Helen, she excused herself and said, "It was nice meeting you. I'll let you be alone with my husband while I go and help Mom with cleaning in the rooming house."

Once Helen disappeared, Pawlo said to Dr. Kozak, "Your mother says you had a difficult time at the university."

"It was the most glaring case of racial discrimination to become a doctor in Winnipeg,"

"How did you reach that conclusion?"

"They have a quota system and the first 50 of 75 openings go to the Anglo's. Slavs and Jews who pass their pre-med exams have a difficult time studying medicine here regardless of their scholastic marks. The rejected reapply each year or apply to the University of Alberta in Edmonton or McGill in Montreal.

Some even take their training in England. As for myself I worked with my father for two years before my application was accepted and when it was, I had thoughts of quitting and should have been in some kind of business."

"Why is that?" Pawlo probed.

"Well, the hazing of medical initiation ceremonies was brutal physically and psychologically. And when I protested to the college against the brutality of the initiation I was tarred, feathered and beaten up so badly that I was hospitalized for three weeks."

"Unbelievable," Petro said.

Dr. Kozak then recalled as initiation approached, the upper class increased the tempo of the preliminary psychological warfare being waged against the freshmen. With nudges to each other while the freshmen looked on, the selected organs of cadavers along with buckets filled with specimens from the pathology laboratory, tidbits were saved in special jars. A group of seniors secretly kneaded Limburger cheese into cigar shapes, which were cut into one-inch lengths and placed in the laboratory incubator to ripen odiferously.

On the night of the initiation, the freshmen were taken to the Arena rink, stripped naked, blindfolded and required to run the gauntlet of two-hundred upper-classmen, armed with paddles for vigorous application, particularly in the case of easily identifiable Jews to the posteriors of the freshmen.

They were next required to roll over ripe-cheese along the floor with their noses, eat pealed grapes, otherwise identified, careen down a children's playground slide into a thankful of blood and intestines from a nearby abattoir into which pails of laboratory specimens were dumped.

After an hour of such horseplay the freshmen were washed down with a fire hose and ultimately allowed to get dressed in clothing pre-treated with itching powder.

Then with a downing of a tumble full of medical alcohol, they were welcomed into the Hippocratic fraternity.

"The ceremony was more hypercritical than Hippocratic, "Dr. Kozak continued, "For it ushered the minority of students into a regiment in which bigoted lecturers never allowed students of the group B class, which was made up of foreigners, to forget that they belonged to an inferior and unwanted race of mankind."

When questioned further about his university days, Dr. Kozak said, "On my application form for instance, I had to list such things as my father's occupation, birth place and religion. And when I handed in my application, the registrar, I remember him glancing at it and noted that my father wasn't an Anglo Saxon. 'Ha,' he said. At least you aren't another Jew. You don't set fires, do you?' a widely belief that all Jews were arsonists and no Jew ever had a fire he had not collected insurance on."

Dr. Kozak continued, "Designing examinations which the minority groups would not pass, I'm certain taxed the imagination of the Examiner also. Students who failed a course were required to repeat it the following year. If they failed the course the second time, they were asked to leave."

Here Dr. Kozak had difficulty speaking but proceeded, "When I flunked in medicine I was told not to try again because I would fail again.

"I refused to take the 'specialists' advice, redid the course, and was at the brink of being failed for the third time when I discovered the instructor was a political bedfellow of Henry Windsor then courting Ukrainians and other ethnic minority for a vote in an election."

Petro encouraged Dr. Kozak to continue.

"Appraised of the situation at the medical college I informed the instructor that if I failed unfairly it would destroy the chances of Windsor winning an election and destroy his credibility among Ukrainian voters. The instructor eventually relented and that's how I got a degree in medicine. My clinic on Selkirk Avenue is becoming a haven for foreign sick people."

"You are fortunate." Pawlo said.

"But my problems weren't over."

"What happened?"

Dr. Kozak's reply was, "During my internship I was taken aside by the Chief of the Medical Staff who said I should consider myself lucky. When asked why he replied that those who intern at the General Hospital are chosen by the size of their charitable donation and intern's father can afford."

"So." Petro said.

"So my father had to borrow money from a bank in order to give a donation."

During September, the school term began with Erin and Margaret teaching in single room schools that were three miles apart. By this time Pawlo and Petro filed their claims at the Land Office for a quarter section of land which cost ten-dollars. Each quarter consisted of one hundred and sixty acres and situated at the outskirts of Winnipeg, adjacent to the Red River. It was land, which the English and French speaking refused to settle on, but had potential for a housing development. Each promised the Canadian government that within three years they would have title to the property after they had made improvements, cultivate some land and have the property fenced.

Having chosen their land, Pawlo and Petro began to tame it as they chopped down trees to build their homes. They sweated under the sun and fought mosquitoes as they cleared trees, dug up roots and rocks and then brought the trees to a nearby sawmill to be made into lumber. As soon as they would find employment, each would build an 18 X 26 single room house that would be plastered with mud and grass on the outside.

The interior would be painted with calcimine. Each house would have a cellar where vegetables, preserves and eggs in a crock filled with water glass were to be kept during winter. The roof would be covered with wooden shingles.

There would be two windows on the south and north sides and one each facing east and west. Calendars would help to decorate the interior and of course there would be a portrait of the Last Supper. There was no kitchen sinks planned but nearby a pail of water would stand on a table covered with an oilcloth.

Next, Pawlo and Petro would each dig and crib a well which aside of providing fresh water to drink, would act as a refrigerator during the summer. Finally an outhouse was to be built where Eaton's catalogue pages used as toilet paper.

Overall the living quarters Pawl and Petro planned wasn't much to endure a harsh winter but still, it was considerably better compared to what earlier East European immigrants had – a dugout. The house built, Pawlo and Petro needed to find a job.

Pawlo initially gained employment by working for Windsor Co. Ltd. at a grocery store, but customers complained about his awkward English and that he smelled garlic, so he was fired.

"Sit down young man!" Windsor roared when Pawlo was called into the office. I'm afraid you no longer can work for the Windsor Company."

"Why, sir?" Pawlo asked as he sat in front of a desk occupied by Windsor.

"For a number of reasons. Customers don't understand you. And…"

"And what?"

"It's the garlic. Hell, you must not only eat it but bathe with the stuff."

Then when Windsor began attacking Ukrainians as well as Jews, Pawlo put his head between his hands and sadly thought, "I see, dear God, please help me."

"Well, anyway, here is the money you have earned thus far and the best of luck in your search for employment elsewhere."

Pawlo pounded the streets of Winnipeg and began to feel frustrated. He wondered if he ever would find employment as he tried to find a job as dishwasher at a hotel, but they laughed at him, as the day before where he had applied as a janitor at Eaton's.

The following day, Pawlo found himself standing outside a building with a sign that read Canadian Pacific Railway and wandered hesitantly inside, where a man stood up from his chair and asked abruptly what Pawlo wanted.

"A job," Pawlo replied, "I'll do anything. Work on the railway. Wait on tables. I need a job desperately."

The man who identified himself as Tom Horne, looked at his pocket watch and then said, "You ever work on the railway before?"

"No, but I'm willing to try."

Horne took a closer look. "How old are you?"

"Twenty."

"You got be twenty-one to work here."

"Then I'm twenty-one. Please. No one will know."

"The boss will kill me if I hire you," Horne groaned and handed Pawlo an application form to fill out. Pawlo noticed that Horne was relenting, so after filling out the form and putting down his age as 21, said, "I'll work hard. I promise I will. Just try me for a few days, a week."

Something told Horne that that Pawlo would work hard. He could tell his supervisor that Pawlo looked over twenty-one.

After examining the application form Horne said, "All right. Come back tomorrow afternoon. One of the men will give you coveralls to wear. You'll be assigned to a gang working on the outskirts of Winnipeg."

Pawlo was overjoyed, "Yes sir. Thank you," he said.

"Be here at four o'clock sharp."

"Yes sir. I promise to be on time."

As Pawlo made his exit, he hoped Horne would not change his mind. On his way to his apartment he ran almost all the way and prayed that Horne's boss wouldn't find out his age, as he would kill Horne.

Petro meanwhile, gained employment as a painter for a construction company.

CHAPTER SIX

During the month of October Erin's school like most grade one to eight schools at the time which was a one-room frame building with plenty of windows on each side.

The basic elements of the room was a table and a chair for the teacher, rows of double desks for the students, a blackboard on the front wall, a picture of the King and Queen of England and above it a Union Jack. A cast iron wood stove supplied the winter heating. Erin would arrive early and start a fire in the stove so that the room would be warm and the ink in the ink bottles on the desk and the drinking water in a pail placed on a table at the rear of the building would have melted during the winter by the time the students arrived.

Outside during recess the children played softball, soccer, pump-pump-pull away, anti-eye over and kick the can or take part in making an afghan that would be ready in time for the Christmas concert in December.

At Margaret's school, where city bred Anglo teachers were reluctant to teach because of a high enrolment of foreigners, the Department of Education was less concerned about afghans then the intellectual content of her class. One day a school inspector visited the school and stayed from 1:00 p.m. until 3:30 watching thirty-five students from grade one to eight go through paces in science, writing, art, composition, history and arithmetic. The children then sang Land Of Hope and Glory, Rule Britannia, and Tipperary. They also recited from memory The Charge of the Light Brigade and The Burial of John Moore.

And when it came to Ukrainian children who spoke little or no English, Margaret wrote the letter A on the blackboard and alongside the letter draw a picture of an apple, pronounce the word, repeat it back and them proceed to the letter B with a picture of a bird. This continued until Z and Margaret draw a picture of a Zebra next to it.

When the school day ended, the inspector found the students attentive and industrious, the work neat and Margaret energetic. The inspector said when the class was dismissed, that he was satisfied with Margaret's teaching but with one exception.

"Is it because of the overcrowded class?"
Margaret asked the inspector.
"No, that isn't the problem,"
"Anxiously, Margaret asked, "What is it
then?"
"It's your vision. I'm afraid we will have to
terminate your employment if it doesn't
improve."
It didn't.

That September, Pawlo, Petro, Erin and
Margaret saw each other frequently and the
girls were invited to a weekend softball game
organized by the Winnipeg Amateur Athletic
Association to promote ethnic understanding.
Pawlo and Petro were to take part in the
game. They were familiar with the game of
soccer but knew little about softball and
hockey, two popular sports in Canada.
A team made up mostly Ukrainian players
played a team made mostly of English
speaking. Initially Pawlo and Petro struck out
because they had never played softball before.
By the fifth inning, however, they got a grasp
of the game and even hit several home runs.

When the game ended the team that Pawlo
and Petro were on defeated the other team by
a score 11-7. The score did not make
members of the opposite team happy and
snide remarks like Scum of Europe, Bohunks,
and Galician's were common.
Pawlo and Petro were used to be called
derogatory names. Even Polish students at
Lvov University called them Bolsheviks, but
that did not bother them.
What did was that a close relationship had
developed with Erin and Margaret, but the
young Irish teachers thought it wasn't the
right time for a permanent one.

Following the game, while the Windsor's
were absent, Pawlo and Petro were invited to
the Windsor home to listen to phonograph
records that Margaret had purchased for an
Edison gramophone earlier in the day. These
included Reuben Roy by Sophie Tucker, Take
Me Out to the Ball Game by Edward Meeker,
In the Good Old Summer Time by Billy
Murray, By the Light of the Silvery Moon by
Ada Jones and Meet Me in St. Louis, Louis
by Billy Murray.

Once inside the Windsor mansion, Pawlo and Petro were awe struck by the grandeur, size and construction, which was mostly of brick and stone. They were surprised too that the Windsor's were absent at the time which gave the two young Ukrainians freedom to gaze at the furnishings and paintings on the wall leading them to believe that the Windsor home belonged to a wealthy and elite Winnipeg family.

While listening to the records the two couples exchanged opinions on different customs in Canada compared to Ireland and Galicia. Erin said that she found it strange that in Canada, at restaurants, people ate chicken with their fingers, to which Margaret replied, "It's better than fighting a chicken wing on your plate with a fork and knife."

"Every country has its peculiarities," Pawlo said. "In Galicia, a common sight in a restaurant is people cleaning their plate with a piece of bread, which they eat afterwards."

"And using a knife while eating fish is a social disgrace," Petro continued.

While discussing social manners Margaret said, "In Canada people shake hands only when introduced.

In Ireland we shake hands with the same person more than once in a day."

"Can you image what happened to me recently?" Pawlo said.

Curios, Margaret said, "What?"

"While at the train station I greeted a man I had not seen for a month, giving him a hug and a kiss. I soon found out that while kissing and hugging a man is a custom in Galicia, it surely isn't in Canada."

"What happened?" Erin asked.

"People nearby laughed. One stranger even asked if I was a faggot."

When the Sophie Tucker record came to an end, Erin changed to Meet Me in St. Louis, Louis by Billy Murray, which was a slow tempo, ideal for dancing. While the two couples were dancing on the oak floor they continued their conversation on the different customs in Canada and Ireland.

About drinking Erin said, "When I first came to Winnipeg I went out with James Buller and he led me to a building with a signs Men and Women. I finally realized that I didn't want to go to the washroom and that man and women didn't drink together.

"So what happened?" Petro asked.

"I said to James 'Forget it.' I still can't get use to the Canadian way that there is something shameful about sharing a drink together as man and woman."

'That is one reason I make my own chokecherry wine and drink at home," Pawlo said and went on, "If I want to have a drink in a public place I go to the Belgian Club in St. Boniface."

"And it's because of places like the Belgian Club that so many women belong to the Women's Temperance League?" Margaret asked.

"The first thing that shocked me about Canada is the politeness of the clerks in stores and the telephone operators," Erin went on. Pawlo disagreed, "Telephone operators? They are okay but not the clerks in the stores."

"What's wrong with the clerks?"

"They always complain Ukrainians smell garlic, but I feel it's a figment of their imagination."

"Well, life in Europe may be more exciting having gone through wars and revolutions but in the end I don't mind the changes in Canada, that is with one exception," Petro said.

Curious, Margaret asked, "What is that?"
"That the English speaking in Winnipeg stop
thinking of Ukrainians as enemy aliens."
After cheek-to-cheek dancing for a short
while, Erin said to Pawlo, "You dance very
well."
Erin said those words even though Pawlo
stepped on her toes several times.
"Petro is the one who dances well, Pawlo
said, "He's good at folk dancing."
"Is that so?" Margaret cut in and asked her
partner for a demonstration.
"I'll dance but only on one condition."
"What's the condition?"
"That the two of you do an Irish Jig and then
sing an Irish song."
"That's not a condition but a pleasure,"
Margaret replied.
Pawlo and Petro advanced to the centre of the
living room floor and without music hurled
themselves into the air. They spun around,
jumped up and down spreading their legs.
They did summersaults and landed on the
floor and then did more acrobatics that
pleased both Margaret and Erin, As soon as
Pawlo and Petro got their breath back Erin
and Margaret took to the floor and did a jig
and then, sang the popular hit of the year 1907
My Wild Irish Rose.

Once the dancing was over, the two couples separated. Pawlo and Erin went to the kitchen while Petro and Margaret remained in the living room where Petro proposed marriage, but Margaret declined and said, "Petro, I probably could love you even if you are of Ukrainian heritage but unfortunately I'm going blind, and if we should get married, I would be a burden to you for the remaining of your life."

"Don't speak that way," Petro protested after Margaret declined marriage because she was going blind.

"I fell in love with you the moment we met on the S S Christiana and you proved your love by lending me five dollars while in Quebec City so that I could stay in Canada. As with your eye disorder, I'm certain an eye specialist that your father recommended will find a remedy."

"No, dear," Margaret replied. "It would be better if you found someone who speaks your language and belongs to the same culture. As for my glaucoma even Dr. Kozak confirms there is no cure and that is why the School Board has terminated my employment."

Petro was greatly disappointed what had happened. First that Margaret had turned down his marriage proposal, and second, that she had been fired by the Winnipeg School Board.

In the kitchen meanwhile Erin said to Pawlo, I would marry you but I'm afraid it would make Uncle Henry unhappy. He has already said, 'Don't throw away your teaching career for a Bohunk. In addition to that, I find James Buller who lives across the street, what can I say, interesting?"

"James Buller? Interesting?" Pawlo said dejectedly. "What have your uncle or James Buller got to do with marrying me? As I told you on the SS Christiana someday I eventually plan to have my own business."

"That's what Uncle Henry is afraid. Privately he told me that you are competitive, enterprising, and full of ideas and prepared to take risks."

"And your uncle says not to even go out with me because I'm Ukrainian?"

"That's the main reason. Uncle Henry says he hasn't met a person who is sympathetic with Ukrainians. They are from his point of view of civilization ten times lower than the Indians."

Pawlo sat down on a couch and placed his hands on both sides of his head and said, "And the Chinese?"

"Them too."

"Those are strong words. Someday I hope to make your uncle eat them. Think about it Erin. You can't measure happiness by your uncle's wealth and his prejudice. Are there other reasons your uncle doesn't want you to marry me?

"There are."

"What are they?"

"He says Ukrainians shelter chickens and pigs in their homes."

"And what else?"

"He says Ukrainians are liars, unwilling to pay their debts and are fond of alcohol."

"Speaking of debts you may be right. I still owe Margaret the five-dollars she lent me while at Immigration and Customs in Quebec City. I agree with the alcohol part too but the rest of your uncle's complains are absurd. You see Erin, we are religious and suspicious. Suspicious that your uncle and Anglo Saxons generally don't understand our historical background.

As far as our marriage is concerned it may take a long time but on the other hand good things are worth waiting for."

As Pawlo and Erin were involved in a love spat conversation, there was a knock on the front entrance door. Erin thought it was her uncle and aunt returning home from the Manitoba Club but that was not so. It was Jimmy McKernan who unexpectedly arrived in Winnipeg from Ireland after having served a three-month prison term in London over Home Rule.
"Welcome to Canada!" Erin greeted her friend and then introduced Jimmy to Margaret, Pawlo and Petro.
After some front talk, Jimmy said, "Erin, look, I've been in prison and am a bit short of money. Can someone lend me several dollars? I'll pay you back as soon as I find employment."
Pawlo came to the rescue and instead of paying the five dollars he owed Margaret, with her approval, handed Jimmy a five dollar bill and Petro added another. "As an immigrant I know what it's like to be broke," Pawlo, said.

"Thank you. Your kindness is much appreciated," Jimmy said and went on, "You may know what it's like to be penniless but you haven't had the experience of being in prison."

"He'll find out if Uncle Henry has his way," Erin said.

"Why?"

"Because Uncle Henry hates Galician's so much that if he had his own way they would all be put into concentration camps."

CHAPTER SEVEN

That week, Jimmy McKernon found employment with the city of Winnipeg. At the time Winnipeggers' were developing various games into a past time and also paid attention to what movie and sports personalities were doing in United States. They followed the careers of Ty Cobb, Babe Ruth and Roger Hornsby in baseball. Boxing also got its attention with names like James Jefferies, Jack Johnson, Tommy Burns and the upcoming Jack Dempsey. Some even thought that City Council meetings were some type of sport.

In summer there was baseball, softball, rugby, cricket, cycling, lawn bowling, tennis and soccer among others. Indoor contests included bowling, snooker and billiards, card games and even dancing contests, which became as arduous as some of the sports.

And in winter there was pleasure skating, speed skating, tobogganing, snow shoeing and of course, hockey. In hockey there were teams for every age group including the Allan and Stanley Cup levels, and commercial leagues for hundreds of players who could not make it with the other teams.

One winter day, Erin said to Pawlo, "Pawlo, I haven't been to a hockey game. What is the game like?"

"Neither have I, so let's go to one this weekend and find out."

St. Boniface

The game Pawlo and Erin chose was in St. Boniface across the Red River.

It was a midget-level game with boys fifteen and sixteen years of age participating between St. Boniface and Winnipeg. In this particular game, St. Boniface supporters sat behind the St. Boniface team and Winnipeg supporters sat behind the one from Winnipeg. Each group came armed with pillows to sit on and all sorts of noise-making devices that included cowbells, sirens and whistles to cheer their team on to victory. It was by sheer accident that Pawlo and Erin sat in the middle of the two groups and had to twist their heads from one end of the rink to the other following the players.

Already Pawlo had heard about hockey stars in the making: Newsy Lalonde, George Hainsworth, the Cook and Patrick brothers, George Hay, Dick Irvin, Joe Simpson, Duke

Keats, Frank Fredrickson and Slim Halderson, among others.

Pawlo and Erin watched the game until near the end of the third period when a fist-fight broke out between two rugged defensemen and then all the players, including the goalies, from both sides got involved punching each other.

"Punching seems more popular than chasing the puck," Pawlo said as the fighting continued.

"The game is too rough for me. It will take at least another fifteen minutes before the referee sorts out the penalties," Erin said.

Pawlo agreed. "Understanding the rules of a hockey game is enough to drive one to drink."

"That's an excellent idea."

"Let's go to the Belgian Club which is down the street."

"Have you been there before?" Erin asked.

"I have. Come, let's go," Pawlo said and away they went.

Liquor law enforcement in St. Boniface was, at best, notoriously casual. The Belgian Club was one of the few dance halls that tolerated open drinking on the premises.

Well brought up Winnipegger's visited there only on a date and never alone. By 11:00 p.m. Pawlo and Erin were demonstrating their dancing talent particularly the foxtrot, Charleston and tango. There was a large sign above a live orchestra that read NO ROUGH DANCING ALLOWED.

What went on in the Belgian Club may not have been sport, under the strict definition of the word, but it was certainly a lot more physically demanding than lawn bowling.

"It's certainly more fun than watching a hockey game," Erin said to Pawlo after each had an alcoholic drink and did more dancing. They drank and danced until 1:00 a. m. when Erin said, "Pawlo, I'm exhausted and feel dizzy."

"Then it's time to go home," Pawlo said and they did, by catching a bus to Winnipeg.

When Pawlo woke up in the morning he picked up a newspaper and read an article where Monsignor Jubinville of the St. Boniface Cathedral lashed out at dancers who frequented the Belgian Club. The Monsignor deplored the spectacle of half-dressed girls writhing around like snakes to the brutal music of jazz.

The Monsignor called their escorts, "Five cent sports that come to mass smelling booze, take Holy Communion and rush out for another bottle."

On the same page of the newspaper, Presbyterians, Methodists and Baptists went even a step further – they supported the Women's Temperance League with the eventual goal of curbing all liquor sales in the Greater Winnipeg area. They demanded prohibition.

CHAPTER EIGHT

Winnipeg - 1911

As the 1911 spring season arrived, the first thing Petro did was erect a cross on his homestead to commemorate the freedom he had found, and then sow wheat on a patch of land he had cleared in the autumn. In another plot near the house, he planted a garden made up mostly of potatoes, cabbages, beans, sunflowers and several rows of poppy seed his mother gave him.

"When the poppy plants ripen I will use their seeds to make loaves of bread like my mother suggested." Petro said to himself. "This is going to be a special occasion marking the freedom we enjoy in Canada and my initiation into Canadian farming."

Before harvest arrived, and due to extreme heat during July and August, the poppies had grown into seed, Petro made his bread and began celebrating his venture into farming. "A meal without poppy seed bread, a spoonful or two of honey and a glass of wine is like a day without sunshine," Petro said to Pawlo and both celebrated.

Petro, however, ate more than he normally would, and when nighttime came crawled into bed and slept longer than usual, because the opium in the poppy seed had taken effect making him drowsy.

When Petro woke up next day, besides having a headache discovered that grasshoppers had destroyed most of the wheat crop he had planted. A month later what crop the grasshoppers didn't destroy an early September frost did.

Petro walked the field and garden to see what damage had been done. The frost on the leaves of the potatoes was turning into droplets of water. The leaves hung limp and lifeless and so were the sunflowers, garlic and cabbages. The carrots, beets and turnips were not affected because their roots were in the ground. Petro knew without looking however, that the wheat he had planted was completely destroyed.

While enjoying breakfast, Pawlo and Petro each assessed their situation. They still had some money left and could butcher a pig as soon as the weather got cold enough and keep the meat frozen when snow came. They could also go hunting, track down deer and bring home venison.

They had money for staples such as flour, lard, oatmeal, sugar, tea and coal oil. To do those things each purchased a .22 caliber rifle so they could also shoot prairie chicken and partridges, and wild animals for their meat and furs. The furs he could sell to the Hudson's Bay Store.

Actually it was a sad time in Petro's life. Due to the crop failure and difficult times, each day he walked his homestead surveying the land from one end of the other. Thoughts of Margaret kept coming to his mind.
It was even a sadder day a short time later, when he picked up his mail and received a three-page letter from his father in Lvov. Most of the pages were used describing the last days before his mother died of pneumonia.

By now, Margaret was getting used to being blind and the fact that she was no longer teaching school implanted on her mind too. One thing was certain – she didn't want to return to Ireland and had to adjust to her lack of proper vision.
When Patricia Windsor said to her, "Margaret without you and Erin I would be the loneliest woman in Winnipeg." she meant it.

When Margaret asked, "Why?" Patricia said, "Your Uncle Henry is wrapped up with the possibility of a war and spends a great deal of his time in Ottawa wishing there was one. John on the other hand, is busy running the grocery business as best as he can and being involved in real estate, doesn't come home until midnight and at times later."

Margaret realized that she was welcome company and assured that she was, when Patricia took her for walks and strolls through the large stores. When the appropriate time came Patricia would read out loud to Margaret and even purchased her a brail typewriter. It was during a reading session that Margaret said, "Aunt Patricia, I'm going to write a book filled with short stories."

Patricia's curiosity was aroused, "And how about a drama?"

"I'm no Bernard Shaw but I will write a drama too."

"And the book of short stories, they will deal with Anglo Saxons living in Winnipeg?

"The stories will deal with Winnipeg but not necessarily Anglo Saxons."

"Then what are you going to write about?"

"Ukrainian women."

"Your stories and drama should be interesting because to be truthful, I find Ukrainian customs and culture difficult to understand."
"Like what?"
"Well, the women wear pretty blouses and bright colors, but their sheepskin coats and babushkas look strange. Don't you think?"
"I admit they are foreigners but not as you put it, strange." Margaret said. "As a matter of fact I find their customs and culture interesting and that's what I'm going to write about. And do you want to know something else?"
This time Patricia said, "What?"
"I'll prove to the Canadian government that blind people can indeed contribute to a growing nation."

Winnipeg- 1911

Pawlo Bilyi, a section man for the Canadian Pacific Railway, joined a craft union. The Industrial Workers of the World and the One Big Union were getting organized but at the time, Pawlo felt that although he belonged to a union he was also a capitalist.

He watched intently as the two top Canadian capitalists, Prime Minister Wilfred Laurier and the leader of the Opposition, Robert Borden, took part in the election process in 1911.

Both, Pawlo and Petro, had read that Laurier had been Prime Minister for almost seventeen years and seemed secure in his office. Laurier was one of the most striking figures on Parliament Hill and often debated with Borden and Windsor many subjects concerning Canada. But not before many weeks had passed, events were to come to a head. There was the question of reciprocity with United States – an arrangement to lower tariffs, which would let primary products, especially wheat, flow south at high prices in exchange for giving Americans a better chance to sell manufactured goods in Canada. Naturally, Eastern Canadian manufacturers opposed any such measure. The move to reciprocity alienated many of Prime Minister Laurier's influential supporters, including the chairman of the Toronto Board of Trade, the president of the Bank of Commerce, Clifford Sifton, the voice of Western Canadian Liberalism, and seventeen other Liberal MP's.

From another quarter came a second challenge. For several years there had been growing concern that the building of German sea power, if not matched, might soon challenge Great Britain's supremacy and security to the empire.

Laurier had hammered out a compromise between those who thought Canada should have something to do with a navy and those who wanted to spend on battleships for Britain. Laurier decided that Canada should create her own small navy.

The following month, Laurier faced the principal foe, Robert Borden, the leader of the Conservatives, who led the party for ten years without much success. Borden with the defection of Sifton and seventeen Liberals came out strongly against the government's proposed reciprocity with United States.

Laurier's second antagonist was Henry Bourassa, a dramatic, competent speaker and a prolific writer who recently found Montreal's Le Devoir newspaper, which usually expressed the majority of opinions of those living in the province of Quebec.

Bourassa too, opposed Laurier's Naval Bill and reciprocity, but on different grounds than Borden did. He was a Canadian and a Quebec nationalist and his cause was to keep Canada and Quebec from the domination by either the English or Americans. For Bourassa, the Naval Bill offered too much to Great Britain and reciprocity, too much to the Americans. The debate over the two contentious issues continued through the winter and spring. Pawlo was surprised that even President Taft of United States got involved in the election and backed Laurier. The surprise turned to shock when the Speaker of the U. S. House of Representatives, Champ Clark, said, "I hope to see the day when the American flag will float over every square foot of the British North American possessions clear to the North Pole."

Pawlo and Petro watched with keen interest as Canadians became so involved in the election that they sang hymns at rallies and the words 'reciprocity' and 'anti-reciprocity', 'tariff' and 'anti-tariff', along with 'Navy for Canada', and 'Battleships for Great Britain', were on everyone's lips. Even author Rudyard Kipling cabled from London as the polls closed on September 21, 1911. Kipling's message read: "It is her own soul that Canada risks today."

When the polls closed, Pawlo and Petro, like many Canadians, were stunned when the election was over. They watched the returns posted outside the office of the *Free Press* newspaper.

When the counting of the ballots was completed, Borden was declared Prime Minister. His Conservatives defeated Laurier Liberals 134 – 87. In Manitoba both Windsor and Sifton were re-elected. Still immigration continued unabated and the economy continued to boom. Optimism was unrestrained and Winnipeg was to be as large as Toronto. Fort George at the head of the Cariboo trail was heralded as the future capital of British Columbia, and Kamloops advertised in Eastern Canada, Europe and United States as the 'Future Los Angeles' of Canada.

At the Canadian Pacific Railway Pawlo found that he worked with different ethnic people: Swedes, Ukrainians, Poles, Russians, and Italians and that his group had at least twelve men, a foreman, a cook and labourers. If drilling through rock was necessary the gang had a driller and a blaster.

The gang that Pawlo was assigned to worked out of Winnipeg and had to build a grade so that it was ready to lie on the track. The gang had to level a strip, fill the grade and then the steel track itself was laid. To dig through the rock the workers used a hammer and a piece of steel. One man held the steel to the rock, turning it slightly after each blow of the hammer while another man above swing the hammer with all his might down on the steel. The hammer swinger got up a regular rhythm; swinging the hammer over his head in a series of blows while other man turned the steel the correct amount during the time the hammer swinger was in motion with a descending for another blow. Most teams changed around, but since Pawl was young and physically strong, he was always the hammer swinger until one day he hurt his back and was about to quit.

"Don't quit," the foreman pleaded. "I'll give you a job tamping railroad ties."

"If I tamp ties how long will it take for me to become a foreman?" Pawlo asked.

"Are you a Galician or a German?"

"I'm Ukrainian."

"And what is your education?"

"I have two years of university.

"If that is the case, you can become a section foreman in a year or two and a road master in ten."

"And to become a superintendent?"

"Being Ukrainian I doubt you'll ever become one."

"In that case, I'm going to quit, as I cannot do physical any longer because of my sore back. In addition to that ten years is a long time to wait."

"If you have a sore back, then I'll let you work in the roundhouse cleaning and firing up locomotives as soon as there is a vacancy," the foreman said.

"Pawlo chose to temp ties until tears rolled down his cheeks and sweat of his browse, but no matter how he pounded the gravel it would often not stay under the ties. The foreman kept saying, "Hurry Mr. Bilyi you are trailing the other employees."

Finally, Pawlo could not work any faster so the foreman grabbed the shovel and handed him a scythe with a crooked handle that was heavier than the shovel, and ordered Pawlo to mow along the railway track.

"If that is the case and you are finding cutting grass and weeds along the track to difficult, you may burn old ties in the ditches or clean up the yard. Which would you prefer?"
"Good. I'll take both," Pawlo said and did.

After work each day, which usually lasted until dark, Pawlo did chores around his boxcar dorm; scribble notes about businesses or read. His favorite magazine at the time was *The Masses*, a weekly Socialist magazine published in New York. Pawlo also enjoyed reading books and within several months read Children of the Poor by Victor Eugene Debs, Zemlya by Emile Zola and Anna Karenina by Tolstoy. Pawlo's favorite Canadian books were *Sunshine Sketches of A Little Town* by Stephen Leacock and *Ann of Three Gables* by Lucy Maud Montgomery. Pawlo also enjoyed reading the *Bible* and each night before going to bed read several chapters. One particular night he turned to Second Corinthians and out loud read Chapter 5, verse, 17, which in part read: "When someone becomes a question, he becomes a new person inside. He is not the same person again."

Then Pawlo flipped several pages and came to the part marked, St Mark, Chapter 29 Verse 23 that dealt with believing all things are possible.

"Inch by inch, anything is a cinch," Pawlo said to himself as soon as he finished reading the passage and began to visualize he was a person equal to any Anglo Saxon in Winnipeg. He would contact Petro to discuss a business. Pawlo then set his Bible aside, blew out the flame of the candle lamp on the table by his bed, and fell asleep

In order to survive Pawlo and Petro had to use all their skills and imagination so one weekend they met at Petro's home. Sitting at a kitchen table they discussed entreprenuring and products they would like to market. Pawlo suggested food and Petro soap. In the end they agreed it would be both as they were necessities in life.

"Pawlo, you are right," Petro said. "I can't imagine anyone going without food."

"And I can't imagine anyone going without a bath," Pawlo replied.

The question now before them, was the type of food and soap to market.

"Of all the food in the world which food should we choose to market?" Pawlo pondered.

"That's easy," Petro replied and following a brief debate both agreed that it should be pyrohy and holubtsi. Pizza wasn't popular at the time.

Next, the two immigrants discussed a sales and marketing plan that was not only simple to follow but rewarded individuals in direct proportion to the amount of effort put into the business.

Pawlo and Petro discussed networking, sometimes referred to as the multi-level accelerated scheme, and not to be confused with the pyramid system where one had to buy from a distributor and only the distributor who originated the scheme made any money. Most distributors would have no selling experience and their goal would be to regularly service customers with pyrohy and holubtsi and a line of soap products and at the same time sponsor distributors.

Pawlo and Petro immediately made a list of everyone they knew – friends, neighbors and fellow workers, people that possibly could be invited into the business and also get referrals.

The plan called for the distributor to purchase a fifty cent KIT that explained the products, the system along with a code of ethics.

"A sponsor will teach a sponsor to market the products," Petro said with enthusiasm. "In other words he or she duplicates themselves to build a firm foundation for a strong and growing business.

"And they have an opportunity to earn extra income on a part-time basis. We will have fun learning together," Pawlo said.

"And earn bonuses. The more products sold the more money a distributor makes," Petro continued.

Pawlo then grabbed a pencil and a sheet of paper and on it, sketched out a marketing plan. Like all distributors one started being sponsored by another distributor and obtaining a sales kit.

One began building their business several ways – merchandising and sponsoring. The gross income was based on product sales. All products were assigned two sets of numbers – the amount of the retail sales and the bonus involved.

For example if the retail sales volume for the month was $20.00 the bonus would be an additional 3%, a sale of $100.00 the bonus would be 6%, $500, 18%, until $1500 worth of products sold where the bonus would remain at 25 percent.

Active distributors who maintained a 25% bonus level for three consecutive months became a Direct Distributor, who qualified for an additional bonus and the right to purchase products direct from the company rather than the sponsor. The Direct Distributor was also invited to attend an exciting expenses-paid trip to Winnipeg for a seminar and the possibility of driving a new model T-Ford through special awards.

"And that's just the beginning," Petro continued. "There are other ways of earning an income too."

"Like what?"

"We'll include a profit sharing bonus," Petro replied and suggested a Ruby bonus equal to 2% of a Direct Distributor's monthly group paid to each Direct Distributor whole monthly personal group sold $3000 worth of products. A pearl bonus equal to 5% of all the second level group down to and including the first qualified Pearl or above personally having sponsored three or more groups which qualified at 25% bonus level in any one month.

A similar schedule of bonuses was worked out when a distributor reached an Emerald, Diamond and a Master distributorship level. The annual year would be from January 1st to December 31st.

Near the end of the meeting, with financial resources stretched to the limit and having discussed all-expense vacations, revenue sharing programs, incentives and personal training of staff, Petro said to Pawlo, "Now we must have a marketing plan looked at by economists. While they are doing that, we must find a location to market our products from."

"That's for sure," Pawlo said and suddenly fear gripped him that he may be doing something he could not handle. To have their own business, caused confusion about Pawlo's and Petro's future. Both were frustrated with their present job and risk was involved.

"Maybe it's time for us to move in a new direction," Pawlo said and Petro agreed with that line of thinking despite having little funding and no experience in selling.

"What will people says when I come calling on them with pyrohy, holubtsi and soap?" "Don't worry what people will say. We will do it together and find out."
There was interesting conversation that afternoon in Petro's home and the two young men ignited an entrepreneurial spirit that could not be dampened. "There is a point in life when one must stop worrying what friends, neighbors, relatives and acquaintances will say. "Petro said.
Pawlo echoed those sentiments when he said, "Why not? What have we got to lose? A little time, perhaps. We are losing time now. Our egos might be hurt, but in the end, I'm certain we are going to end with a dynamic corporation."

CHAPTER NINE

Winnipeg - 1912

Pawlo continued to date Erin and Petro, Margaret. Petro earlier said that it was a frustrating that Margaret did not want to marry him at this time.

A tragedy the entire world would remember forever took place the following April. Erin read the tragic newspaper article to her pupils the following day. "Yesterday the largest ship in the world, Titanic, on its maiden voyage from England to New York struck an iceberg off Newfoundland and sank. The catastrophe took 1,517 lives."

The date the Titanic sank was April 15, 1912.

The following day, prayers were held in St. Basil's Catholic Church for the Titanic victims. Most Ukrainians were either Greek Catholic or Orthodox. Pawlo and Petro embraced the Greek Catholic faith, communion with the Roman Catholic Church, but retain its own liturgy and separate organization.

When the prayers ended, Pawlo and Petro introduced Erin and Margaret to Father Dymytro Patrushka, a temporary fill-in from United States and Erin said to the priest, "That was a wonderful service, Father. It means so much to Margaret and me because many of the Titanic victims were of Irish ancestry."

Among prominent Americans who drowned were John Jacob Aster, Isidor Straus and Francis Millet, the painter. A prominent Canadian was Charles Melville Hays who was a commissioner with the Grand Trunk Railway and prominent in Winnipeg. When Erin asked Father Patrushka why he looked tired he did not hesitate, "Because there aren't enough Catholic priests in Winnipeg to take care of our people."

"Why is that?"

"Because attempts to interest priests who are subsidized by the government in Austria, have been unsuccessful."

"Why?" Erin kept probing. "Even if the Canadian government gave the priests a salary?"

"That was suggested by Dr. Olesciw but it was turned down."

Petro joined in the conversation and asked, "Why?" and was told, "The Canadian government said it was an unprecedented request and refused."

"Then how about the French, Belgian and Irish priests? Can't they do something?"

"Priests from foreign countries do not understand our Catholic rites; consequently they cannot minister our needs."

With that part Pawlo agreed. The last time I went to confession the Belgian priest gave me for penance five Our Father's, five Hail Mary's and a Gloria Be."

Father Patrushka burst out with laughter."

"What's so funny?" Margaret asked.

"That's nothing. I know one couple that asked the foreign priest to have food blessed, as they had been accustomed in the Old Country. The priest who was Irish and the couple did not speak each other's language, so the couple simply held out the bread, eggs, milk and cheese to be blessed. The kind priest thought it was a kind of an offering and began helping himself to the food, where upon the couple that was poor, quickly seized the food that was left and ran home."

On December 19, 1912 the first Bishop of the Ukrainian Catholics arrived in Winnipeg from Ukraine. Nykyta Budka's (1877-1949) tasks were monumental as his diocese stretched from the Pacific to the Atlantic Oceans and encompassed approximately 150,000 Ukrainians and approximately 80 churches and chapels. Initially there were 13 secular priests and 9 monks, including the Bishops secretary, Reverend Joseph Bala, who accompanied him to Canada from Ukraine, assisting in the service of this wide expanse of faithful and organized communities. Bishop Budka's work focused mainly on visiting the faithful and organizing new parish communities.

Winnipeg - 1913

In 1913 the unification was completed, but the Bishop who had the potential of becoming a saint, wasn't familiar with Canadian affairs and in Winnipeg, urged his followers to return home and fight for Austria, although he retracted the letter later.

This resulted in more prejudice and war hysteria among the Anglo Saxon population.

It also caused embarrassment not only to Pawlo and Petro, but eventually humiliation and suffering to most Ukrainians in Canada. Between 1897 and 1912 over one-half million people came to Canada from Europe. Of that amount 170,000 came from Galicia and settled mostly around Winnipeg, Dauphin and Edmonton.

While Pawlo continued working for the Canadian Pacific Railway, Petro discussed with chemists a formula for soap and with lawyers and accountants, the marketing strategy for selling pyrohy and holubtsi. Construction at the time was booming and the Federal Government restrictions on Oriental Immigration caused railway companies to turn to southern and eastern Europeans for cheap labor. Later, however, the economy began to turn into a recession and Pawlo was one of the first to feel its effects – he along with hundreds of immigrants got released from their jobs and began to congregate on Winnipeg streets. The boom had turned to bust.

"Good heavens, what gives? This is getting to be more and more like conditions in the Austria-Hungarian Empire," Pawlo said to Nathan Tarnoff, a Jewish storekeeper in the North-end of Winnipeg where Pawlo and

Petro often shopped. Both preferred to shop with Jewish merchants and peddlers than those of Anglo or French origin. This was not surprising because many of the Jews came from Eastern Europe, spoke their language, and were familiar with Galician idiosyncrasies.

Among the usual problems of being Jewish in Winnipeg, however, was to maintain his dietary rules under frontier conditions.

In Winnipeg, tension was rising. Lower in scale even than the despised Galician's from the Austria-Hungarian Empire were the Jews who were rock bottom on the Anglophone pecking order and would have been without the language or the garlic problem. The binding mortar of Judaism was religious and not language. And it was Judaism that gave Protestants and Catholics of all shakes their common denominator – anti-Semitism.

Pawlo, however, publicly said, "Jews are more than storekeepers; they are interpreters, counselors and trusted friends."

This was true because Jewish stores became informal gathering places and it was at such a gathering that Pawlo found out Tarnoff was moving to Chicago.

Taking Pawlo to one side and in privacy,
Tarnoff said to him, "Pawlo, I want you to
know that I'm moving to Chicago. With a
small down payment I'll carry the mortgage,
if you and Petro want to buy my store."

"You are moving to Chicago? Has it got
anything to do with anti-Semitism?" Pawlo
asked.

"That and because our son, Abraham, has
been refused to enter the Winnipeg College of
Medicine for the third time."

"And how about your other son, Nathan Jr.?
How is he doing at the University of Alberta
in Edmonton?"

"Nathan will graduate in business
administration next May and says he will look
for a career in America instead of returning to
Winnipeg."

Pawlo and Petro were realistic that banks
didn't talk to women, so they consulted with
Dr. Kozak while Margaret and Erin listened.
In a bold decision Pawlo and Petro were
convinced to open an account at a bank and
apply for a loan which Dr. Kozak would co-
sign and Pawlo's and Petro's parcels of land
used as collateral.

Once the loan was approved, Pawlo and Petro
not only bought the Tarnoff General Store,
which had living quarters with two bed rooms
on the second story, but also some of the
contents as well.

The Tarnoff General Store was a white
colored wood frame building with a red-
shingled roof. The walls were worn in places
and paint peeling. Inside oiled floorboards
smelled of dust and linseed oil. The store sold
feed and fuel, groceries and clothing. The
interior featured hand-written signs
advertising goods found on wooden shelves.
There were no surveillance systems because
Tarnoff and his family lived upstairs and
shoplifting was rare.
From the first day the store ownership
changed, Pawlo and Petro were a success.
What they did was to manufacture Ukrainian
favorites – pyrohy and holubtsi along with a
variety of soap and began mass marketing the
products.

The store also served as a retail outlet in the
general grocery line – meat, milk, coal oil,
lard, sugar, ice cream and oatmeal.

"With our exclusive marketing plan every home in Winnipeg will soon enjoy one of our products," Pawlo said in an interview with the *Free Press* and *Ukrainian Voice* newspapers. What Pawlo and Petro had done was to initiate their network distributorship plan that had been approved by accountants and lawyers, and began manufacturing pyrohy and holubtsi in one part of the store and rented a nearby warehouse to manufacture the soap.

The manufacturing was done under the name MANCAN -- Man meaning a human being and Can that the same human being can reach a dream if he/she sets their mind to do it. At first it was only a dream, but now their plan was taking shape. Pawlo and Petro felt their products were the best on the market and included a guarantee that if anyone weren't satisfied the customer would get a full refund. What Pawlo and Petro had done was to prepare a sales kit outlining the marketing plan and how to sponsor other distributors. And they got into both right away by renting the Ukrainian National Hall and inviting neighbors, acquaintances, fellow workers and their friends that possibly could be interested into going into business for themselves.

The meeting would explain how the marketing plan worked, the opportunities the business had for growth and how distributors could make money and become financially secure.

Those who came to the meeting came in all sizes, shapes and forms and ages.
Some were educated and some weren't. There were males and females and most of those who spoke a foreign language and from all walks of life. There were schoolteachers, doctors, union members, prohibitionists and people in wheel chairs. There were farmers, athletes, bus drivers, electricians, accountants, clerks, railway workers and the unemployed.
"I wanted information on how to be self-employed and earn a little cash in my spare time," said a receptionist at the General Hospital waiting for the meeting to begin, and when it did, it was 8:00 p. m. sharp with the hall three-quarters filled. This is when Pawlo waked up to the podium, placed in the middle of a stage and politely said, "Attention please, it's time for the meeting to begin."
A large poster stretched across the back wall that read THE MANCAN CORPORATION and underneath the words The Canadian Way to First Rate Products and Security.

Upfront of Pawlo was a display of Mancan products that included pre-cooked packaged pyrohy, holubtsy, and soap ranging from laundry detergent to hair shampoo, neatly packaged.

Pawlo first spoke about how the idea of Mancan Corporation got started and why the products were so good, if not superior, to those presently on the market by competitors. "Competitors? There are no competitors," Pawlo said describing the pyrohy and holubtsi. They are pre-cooked and come in packages of twelve. All you do is pop them into boiling water and three minutes later enjoy them.
The pyrohy come in six different flavors: potato, blueberry, Saskatoon, plum, raspberry and cottage cheese. In the holubtsi we use homegrown Winnipeg cabbage, rice and our secret spices. They are made the way you want them made. They are delicious."

Next, Pawlo turned to the soap products. Picking up a package nearest to him, he continued, "Mancan X for instance is complete laundry soap not available in any of the Windsor stores because we developed it.

It cleans better than any other leading brand because the soap contains more grease fighters, special cleaner and stains fighters. The buildup in water conditioners increase cleaning power and the corrosion inhibitor protects your laundry tub or washing machine if you are fortunate to have one. At any rate your clothing, including the old man's socks, comes out sparkling clean."

Next Pawlo stepped to a table conveniently placed in front of him and gave a demonstration of Mancan products that appeared to impress everyone. This included demonstration of Mancan Premium soap for the face and bath. Mancan Standard, for the dishes. Mancan Commercial, for use in factories. There was also a full line of Mancan Shampoo, Mancan toothpaste, a Mancan deodorant and Mancan cosmetics.

Once Pawlo convinced those present that Mancan products indeed were superior to what competitors offered, continued, "As time moves on we at Mancan Corporation plan to introduce homecare, person care health products and even merchandise products found in Eaton's catalog. Who knows, in the future we may market cars, long distance telephone service and flights to the moon."

Next, Pawlo introduced Petro as his partner, co-founder and president of Mancan Corp. and went on, "Petro Czorny will now explain how the Marketing Plan works."

As those present applauded Petro walked up to a blackboard that was set to one side earlier, picked up a chalk and drew a circle. "And now these are the people you sponsor," he said. To simplify the procedure and not confuse potential distributors Petro spoke slowly and invited questions.

"First, you must remember that the basic commission on whatever you sell, is roughly 30% of whatever you sell and there are additional bonuses from three to twenty-five percent.

For example if you sell $20.00 worth of products you get to keep six dollars and a bonus of three percent, which is sixty cents for a total earning of $6.60 or annualized for a gross income of $79.20. I'm certain each one of you could use $7.20. Couldn't you?"

There was an "Aha" response from those present.

"And now if we help you to sponsor six distributors and they each sell twenty dollars' worth of products in the month, the income for the seven of you will be how much?"

Petro paused and waited for an answer to make certain those present were following the marketing strategy. He also knew that everyone was going to do his or her mathematics.

"That makes it $46.20 each month or $554.40 a year!" someone from the audience hollered.

"And now suppose the six people you sponsored, sponsored six more. Can you imagine the income? And if the six sponsored six more?"

Someone from the audience shouted, "Then I'll have to hire an accountant."

The comment drew laughter from the crowd. Petro then talked about a Sales Kit, a requisite to be a Mancan distributor, and an application form found inside the kit.

When Petro was through speaking, Pawlo joined him at the podium and invited questions from the floor, which weren't many. Having to answer only several questions Pawlo knew he had aroused enough interest for most of those present to become distributors of Mancan. This was confirmed when a woman sitting in the middle the second row said, "Sign me up."

And another voice said, "Me too."

Still another, "That includes me."

Then a woman more enthusiastic than the other voices said, "Here's an opportunity for a new lifestyle. I challenge anyone to sign more distributors than I can within ninety days."

The opportunity to earn extra income on a part-time basis and to sponsor other distributorships caught on. Ninety-two of the one hundred and forty three people present purchased their Mancan Sales Kit that night. A woman in a wheelchair identified herself as Maria Tiahlo pulled up to Petro and said, "My initial goal is to service ten customers once a month. As I see it customer service is the lifeblood of the business. Mancan could mean profitability. It will be fun to teach other distributors."

Maria Tiahlo then introduced Petro to a neighbor of hers, Paraska Orelesky, stout and pretty, and about the same age as Petro.

Paraska did not speak English well but said to Petro that her parents lived not far from where Petro lived.

"Just up the Red River," she said. "I'm Tony Orlesky's daughter."

Turning to Maria Tiahlo, Petro asked, "What is your personal reason in joining Mancan?"

Mrs. Tiahlo clung to her wheelchair and said, "To be honest, the extra cash will provide me with just enough money for my daughter to take piano lessons."

Another prospect that identified herself as Victoria Jackson and spoke English well, walked up Pawlo and said, "I have purchased a Mancan Sales Kit. Pyrohy (dumplings) and holubtsi (cabage rolls) in packets of twelve and six distinct flavors appeals to me. In time they will be more popular than hot dogs. Watch me; I'll even have Henry Windsor, our Tory MP, enjoying them although he detests Ukrainians."

As the Mancan Corporation began to grow, so did the distributors' enthusiasm. Within several months Mancan became a rival to the Windsor Stores throughout Winnipeg.

CHAPTER TEN

Winnipeg - 1914

At his home in Winnipeg, Henry Windsor tried to have a nap but couldn't sleep.

It was a humid Saturday July 1914, several minutes before supper was to be served and a culmination of a hectic week of debate in Ottawa. The debate dealt with the sighting of German dreadnaughts along the west coast of British Columbia but the 'Rainbow' was unable to find them. Canada not having a navy of its own bothered Windsor, but his Tory government had other problems to contend with too: high unemployment, railways losing money and strikes throughout the country.

A War Book of Plans for each branch of the government was just completed and Windsor instead of sleeping was reading it. He always thought Canada should have military training on the Swiss model. If militarism was state of mind or a set of values that supported patriotism, it wasn't the case with his wife, Patricia and Margaret and Erin who entered the den where Windsor was supposed to have been napping.

"There, I told you so. Besides aliens Ukrainians are liars," Windsor said to Patricia after earlier reading an account of Bishop Budka's stand on the Austro-Hungarian Empire loyalty in the *Free Press* newspaper. "What this country needs is a bill that will make it difficult for Ukrainians to obtain naturalization papers."

"Is that why the British Nationality Naturalization Bill is about to be passed by Parliament?" Erin asked.

"The bill will certainly help to make Canada predominantly Anglo Saxon." Windsor replied and urged both Margaret and Erin to apply for Canadian citizenship as soon as possible.'

"We'll do that, "Margaret said. "Thank you for the reminder."

Margaret was fascinated with her uncle's point of view. "And like in the Austro-Hungarian Empire you would have newspapers printed only in one language?"

"That's right. English only," Windsor said. "All foreign publications must be monitored by the government."

"And how about the Trades and Labor Congress whose unions may soon strike for higher wages?"

"The Trades and Labor Congress is a left wing organization which could lead Canada into ruin. If I had my way I'd put the leaders into prison."

"But Uncle Henry," Erin cut in. "Canada is a country that prides itself in freedoms. Freedom of speech, freedom of the press, freedom of assembly. I could go on and on. Canada is supposed to be the Promised Land."

"Speaking of promises, when will parliament give women the right to vote?" Patricia cut in.

"Yes, Uncle Henry, what have you got to say about that?" Margaret joined in.

Voting rights for women was not a topic Windsor wanted to discuss so Margaret brought up the subject of children taken from workhouses and orphanages in Britain and sent to Canada to work on farms.

"Like Galician immigrants they are often cruelly treated, but Britain says good riddance. The children are powerless to fight back," Margaret said.

Between 1869 and 1910, 60,000 British children were sent to Canada. In the next 20 years another 27,000 arrived but these children did not concern Windsor.

His reply was, "At least these children are of good character whish more than I can say for Ukrainians."

Further in the conversation Windsor said, "Ukrainians are Bolsheviks who read the *Ukrainian Voice* newspaper always hoping for an independent Ukraine. If that's what they want then why do they come to Canada?"

Margaret's reply was, "Because Ukrainians like the Irish are governed by a ruthless power. Ukrainians by the Austro-Hungarian Empire and Russia, and Ireland by England. Come to think of it Uncle, why did you come to Canada if it wasn't freedom?"

At that precise moment there was a knock on the door and rather answering Margaret, Windsor didn't acknowledge the question. Instead he decided to answer the call. When he opened the door, petite and pretty Anglophone by the name of Victoria Jackson was standing in front of him.

"Good evening Mr. Windsor, Ms. Jackson said. "My name is Victoria Jackson from Jackson Marketing International.

"The company has asked me to stop by and share with you what we are doing in Winnipeg. It will take five to fifteen minutes; perhaps we can do it now?"

By his facial expression Ms. Jackson realized, Windsor didn't know what to say or do, so within seconds, she put her foot inside the door, which drew Windsor to answer, "Certainly, why not? Please come inside."

As Windsor led Ms. Jackson to the living room table, she noticed a painting hanging on the wall and said, "Sir, that looks like a valuable piece of art. You must have purchased it in Paris?"
To set the stage for selling Jackson began establishing common ground between Windsor and her, art, and began to control the direction of the meeting by listening and questioning. Ms. Jackson thought this will give Windsor an opportunity to boast, and he did, when he politely answered, "This particular piece of art was purchased in Paris and there's none like it in Winnipeg."
Jackson's knowledge about art was limited however, so she asked additional questions about Windsor's family and his trips to Ottawa. Since Windsor's prime occupation was political in nature, she then asked, "Do you think there's a possibility of a war?"
"Possibility? The way the world situation is at present it should be here, mark my word, any moment."

As soon as Ms. Jackson got three positive "Yes's" or nods, she continued with her presentation. "Mr. Windsor, Jackson Marketing International has affiliated itself with the Mancan Corporation.

"This affiliation enables you to share in large discounts and services that competitors are unable to provide. For instance, we market pyrohy and holubtsi plus a full line of soap that I would like to show you."

"Pyrohy, holubtsi and soap," Windsor said. "That's quite a combination. I doubt we need any of that Ukrainian stuff. Soap? Let me call my wife who is in the kitchen. Hey, Patricia!"

As soon as Patricia came, Ms. Jackson introduced herself and Patricia in turn introduced Margaret and Erin. Following the introductions Ms. Jackson said, "The pyrohy and holubtsi come in six different flavors and easy to serve. You pop them in boiling water for three minutes and enjoy them. They are delicious."

Windsor's curiosity was aroused when Jackson pulled out a packet from her demonstration kit

Erin and Margaret did not say a word because they realized that Ms. Jackson was a distributor of Mancan products, which Pawlo and Petro co- found and if Windsor was aware of this, he would take a tantrum fit and not purchase any of the products. In the end Windsor purchased ten packets of pyrohy, mostly blueberry and plum flavor, and six packets of holubtsi. Then Ms. Jackson went into the soap demonstration and Patricia took over from her husband.

"When it comes to washing clothes I'm the one who does the purchasing," Patricia said. In the end Patricia purchased soap for the laundry, bathroom, along with a bottle of hair shampoo, a tube of toothpaste and a jar of under arm deodorant.

Before Ms. Jackson left, Patricia asked, "Would you like to enjoy ad cup of tea with Erin, Margaret and me?"

"I'd like that," Ms. Jackson said and within the next hour had two referrals, both in the Windsor neighborhood. By the time the evening was over Jackson sold $8. 00 worth of goods and sponsored a customer.

Victoria Jackson did what everyone else thought was impossible, she had Windsor hooked on Ukrainian pyrohy and holubtsi.

Erin seemed to lead a life of luxury when a week after Ms. Jackson made her sale to the Windsor family and Pawlo watched as Erin and James Buller enter the Walker Theatre, renounced for its splendor and concerts.

"Erin is stepping out on me," Pawlo said disappointedly to himself about his wavering love affair with Erin.

The presence of Erin with a competitor made Pawlo, if not jealous, heartbroken. He went to his the Mancan Store living quarters and imbibed in chokecherry wine, which he made the year before. After several drinks Pawlo leaned out the second story window muttering to himself, "Erin, Erin, Erin…." His abuse of the English language and the use of an excessive alcoholic drink offended several people who passed on the street level.

One of the pedestrians was a member of the Women's Christian Temperance Union who invariably linked foreigners; alcohol and politicians in a class of corruption and degradation, expressed an opinion when she saw Pawlo in an inebriated condition.

Pointing a finger upward at Pawlo she shouted, "You sir, are an unfortunate product of civilization that is a thousand years behind the Canadian."

Pawlo reminded himself of the Anglo-Saxon criticism of his people. Earlier in the day he had read an editorial in the Free Press that in part read: "There are a few people who believe that Slav immigrants are desirable settlers or that they are welcomed by white people in Western Canada.

Those whose ignorance is impenetrable, whose customs are repulsive, whose civilization is primitive and whose character and morals are justly condemned are surely not the class of immigrants which the country paid immigration agents to see and attract. Better by far, to keep our land for the children and children's children than fill up the country with the scum of Europe."

The thought of Erin, if he was Caucasian or not, and the effect the chokecherry wine made Pawlo sleep longer than usual.

He was late in opening the Mancan Store that day, but that did not matter, what did was that Mancan distributors were clamoring for more pyrohy, holubtsi and soap products.

During the time that Petro farmed, besides his interests in Mancan, he developed a circle of friends who spoke his own language.

The thoughts of Margaret becoming a burden to him ran through his mind frequently Often he debated with himself, if he should forget Margaret and marry one of his kind, "One has to give Margaret credit for her honesty," Petro said.

In the end, however, Petro struck up a relationship with Paraska Orlesky whose parents homesteaded next to Petro and whom he met at the first Mancan meeting.

Petro got to know Paraska better when he broke more land on the homestead with a pair of oxen that he borrowed from Paraska's parents.

The oxen were powerful and enduring. They posed problems in addition to those encountered with horses which most of the neighbors used. The oxen needed a lot of hay, oats and water; they were slow and dribbled their tongues in the heat of summer. And like humans oxen didn't like the black flies and mosquitoes that plagued the countryside.

One day while breaking land, the oxen spotted a path that led to the Red River and no perseverance would prevent them from going into it. Every round the oxen made, they invariably wanted to head towards the river.

Petro found it quite a chore, not only to stop the oxen heading for the river, but once they got there to turn them back. Finally Petro had to resort to place Paraska on the path with a pitchfork to signal to the animals that it was definitely to their favor to keep plowing the land and not to head for the river. Petro however, felt sorry for the oxen and Paraska said, "I know how the oxen feel."

Curious, Petro said, "How?"

"Like Ukrainians living in Canada. They find endurance to perform in heat and discomfort while carrying an unyielding burden of a heavy yoke."

As time went on Petro sponsored more friends and acquaintances into Mancan, broke more land, seeded more wheat, added other vegetables and herbs. Then one week following a heavy rain the Red River rose and eventually burst its banks.

"Right now I wish I lived in Lvov," Petro said to Paraska as he counted his farm losses.

"You can't do anything but watch."

Petro, like most of his neighbors ignored the flood and stayed behind to protect his property. "I can't give up now. Paraska and I fought this river night and day.

No way. We'll keep plugging ahead," Petro said to Pawlo who came to see the damage done and suggested that he and Petro quit farming, and pay more attention to the administration of the Mancan Corporation.

"I admit it's very depressing, standing watching and seeing a life-time saving float down the river, "Paraska said while squeezing Petro's hand. At the precise moment Paraska noticed a wheelchair bound woman in difficulty while vacating her nearby premises fronting the Red River.

"My God!" Paraska screamed. "That's our Mancan distributor friend Maria Tiahlo!"

As soon as Paraska said those words, she jumped into a canoe and paddled furiously toward Maria.

Petro's plea, "Hey, Paraska! Come back or else you will drown!" came too late. The canoe capsized and the torrid current of the Red River swept Paraska's body towards Lake Winnipeg.

And soon as Petro stopped grieving for Paraska and the water of the Red River receded, he and Pawlo each had an offer from Windsor Company Ltd. to purchase their homesteads.

John Windsor who acted as agent said to them, "Mr. Bilyi and Mr. Czorny, you each paid ten dollars for one-hundred and sixty acres of land, but since you made improvements I'll each give you five hundred."

It was an offer Pawlo and Petro could not resist. With the money they paid off the balance of the Tarnoff mortgage and instead of renting, purchased outright the nearby warehouse.

The only one to make an immediate fortune however, was John and Henry Windsor, who subdivided the properties into lots. Windsor Co. Ltd. besides operating a chain of stores, soon became known as Real Estate Kings of Winnipeg, where its head office near Portage and Main was the scene of daily and nightly lot auction sales. The Windsor's sold so many River Front and View lots within several months that they became millionaires, second time over.

"We'll celebrate our fortune and the stupidity of the Ukrainians selling their land so cheaply by having a champagne bath, John Windsor said to his father as soon as the senior Windsor returned to Winnipeg from Ottawa for a weekend.

The two Windsor's had their bath but land speculation could not last forever.

The day the Windsor's were having their champagne bath, Archduke Ferdinand, heir to the thrones of Austria and Hungary, was assassinated together with his wife in Sarajevo, Yugoslavia.

The assassin, Gavarilo Princip was an agent for the Serbian terrorist organization, Bland Hand.

The assassination was on the same day Pawlo and Petro each received a letter from the Austrian vice-consul in Canada to report to the Austrian army. In part the letter read: "Amnesty for draft dodgers will be granted."

After reading the letter Pawlo said in disgust, "If I join an army it will be a Canadian army."

"Here, here," Petro said. "That goes for me too. And if not the Canadian army then it will be the British. Certainly it won't be the Austrian army, since the Serbs are Slavs and Slavic people have fought Austrians over 400 years."

In Canada meanwhile, the federal government was about to pass the British Nationality Act, which would strip many immigrants of their citizenship.

Immediately after the Archduke's assassination the war crises in the summer of 1914 boiled up with incredible speed. First Austria declared war on Serbia, and then Germany declared war on Russia, Belgium and France. President Wilson of United States declared, "America will remain neutral." "Britain certainly will not enter the war," Patricia said to her husband the same day. "And if she does it will be over by Christmas."

The comment enraged Windsor to the point that he dropped a Union Jack flag he was admiring and began pacing the floor wondering when it would.

Ottawa – August 1914

Near midnight August 4, 1914 Windsor had the answer when Britain and her Dominions declared war on Germany.

"When Britain is at war Canada is at war," Windsor said next morning quoting former Prime Minister Laurier.

As soon as Windsor had eaten his breakfast, he packed his suitcases full of clothing and took the next scheduled train to Ottawa for an emergency session of parliament.

He did not leave, however, before he got assurance that his son John would enlist in the army.

"Good boy! Good boy! We'll show the Krauts," the senior Windsor said and when John assured his father that he and James Buller had talked about enlisting several hours earlier, he was ecstatic.

Meanwhile, right across Canada (population 7.2 Million) newspapers flashed the headline: Canada Declares War on Germany, and news vendors hollered, "Extra! Extra! Read all about it!"

Three days later, while Windsor was in Ottawa, the Federal Government with the encouragement of Prime Minister Borden, passed the first in a series of laws that curtailed normal rights and freedoms for German and Austrian immigrants. A week later still, legislation was introduced giving local police the right, without Any Particular Evidence to imprison or detain anyone who attempted to leave the country or assist the enemy.

While MP Windsor was in Ottawa, a mass meeting took place in the Board of Trade auditorium in Winnipeg, to protest Bishop Budka's pastoral letter, which he retracted but the damage had been done. The Bishop had reminded his parishioners of their allegiance to the Austro-Hungarian Empire and enlist in the Austrian army. The bishop was openly attacked from many quarters, including Ukrainian ones, as a traitor to Canada. Manitoba's Liberal Provincial Administration was most adamant about having the bishop deported. Bishop Budka was arrested and charged several times, but because lack of evidence, the charges against him were withdrawn. Overworked and tired, the bishop had laid the foundations for the Ukrainian Catholic Church in Canada never the less.

The man who could get himself and his community into so much trouble was also a man who would stay up all night with a Ukrainian sentenced to hang, minister to him and then walk with him to the gallows. In addition to having his work as Bishop severely hampered, because of all the tumult, the Canadian government decided to intern Ukrainians as suspicious and potentially treacherous foreigners living in Canada. "Nonsense," Pawlo said to the overflowing crowd. "Bishop Budka, although he appeared to warn his people about Russian designs on their land, and later appealed to Ukrainian

Canadians to stand up for the British Empire, is a stupid mistake, although the Bishop realizes his mistake. A lot of damage has already been done."

Most Ukrainian leaders present, were members of either, the Russian Orthodox, Greek Orthodox, Ukrainian Catholic or Greek Catholic faith, and a rift over church matters, themselves agreed with Pawlo and Petro. It was not surprising when the meeting ended that Anglophone Canadians stood outside the auditorium shouting derogatory phrases like, "Scum of Europe." "Enemies of Canada", "Bishop Budka and all Germans, Austrians and Galician's should be deported."

That evening, when Pawlo and Petro returned to the Mancan General Store, they found the building painted with anti-ethnic slogans. Hope You Choke on Your Pyrohy and Holubsi was a prominent graffiti. Another read: Anyone Using Mancan Products Is a Communist and still another was Galician's Should Be Deported or Interned.

A block further, those who wrote the slogans stood at attention singing God Save the King; at about the same time, a group in Montreal was singing La Marsellaise.

Politicians of whatever stripe or region were almost unanimous. Even Bourassa wrote in the Le Devoir that it was Canada's duty to contribute within her strength and means, which are proper to her to triumph, and especially to the endurance, of the combined efforts of France and England.

On August 21, 1914 Windsor stood up in the House of Commons and said to Prime Minister Borden, Please make absolutely certain you omit no power that the government may need."

The following day, August 22, 1914, the War Measures Act was passed and gave the federal government full authority to do everything deemed necessary "for the security, defence, peace, order and welfare of Canada."
It could be used when the government thought that Canada was about to be invaded or war would be declared, in order to mobilize all segments of society to support the war effort.

The act also gave the federal government sweeping emergency powers that allowed the Cabinet to administer the war effort without accountability to Parliament, and without regard to existing legislation.

It gave the government additional powers of media censorship, arrest without charge, deportation without trial, expropriation, control and disposal of property. This Act was always implemented via an Order in Council, rather than approval of the democratically elected Parliament.

By world standards Canada is a country that respects and protects its citizens' human rights. That has not always been true, however.

The War Measures Act, statue (1914) met the test and permitted the federal cabinet to make decisions by order-in-council and prohibited enemy aliens from leaving their homes or being near bridges, waterway and railroads. The act also gave police the right to search for weapons, and when they did, Petro and Pawlo turned in their 22-caliber rifle that they used to shoot animals and birds as a source of food when they first arrived in Canada.

When Pawlo, who by now made up with Erin, asked, "What is an order in council?" she replied, "That's when a prime minister becomes a dictator."

Throughout all this, Prime Minister Borden promised immigrants from countries at war with Canada. They would be protected from abuses that would result from wartime hysteria. Borden assured immigrants from Germany and regions under the Austro-Hungarian Empire from which majority of Ukrainians came, that as long as they did nothing to aid the enemy, "They were entitled to the protection of the law. Because the immigrants were invited to become citizens of this country and we owe it to them, in trying circumstances in which we are placed, the duty of fairness and consideration."

But the public did not go for the government's policy of tolerance. Business and labor groups, mostly Anglo Saxons and in Western Canada, demanded that enemy aliens, either immigrants or nationalized Canadians, to be dismissed from their jobs and thrown into internment camps

Some asked that a one-thousand dollar head tax be placed on any new immigrant from Eastern Europe.

Miners in Alberta and British Columbia went on strike until the company they worked for fired all German and Austrian employees.

Ottawa – October 1914

In October 1914 another order-in-council was passed which permitted twenty-four concentration camps across Canada. (Later called internment camps) including camp #10 in Brandon, Manitoba. The camps were supposed to house enemy alien immigrants who had contravened regulations or who were deemed to be security threats.

In fact, the "enemy aliens" could be interned if they failed to register, or failed to report monthly, or traveled without permission, or write to relatives in the Austria-Hungarian Empire. Other less concrete reasons given for internment included "Acting in a very suspicious manner" and being "undesirable."

This is the time Pawlo and Petro became concerned about their safety even more than they were before. Registration offices were being opened by Dominion Police in Eastern Canada and the North West Mounted Police in the western part where most of the Germans and Galician's lived.

Canadian men meanwhile, were encouraged to enlist into the Canadian army.

John Windsor and James Buller who enlisted in Winnipeg's 28th Canadian Infantry

Battalion spent the first winter billeted in an old structure called the Horse Show Building. In the absence of bunks, the volunteers slept as they could, on sawdust and manure covering the floor of the arena.

There was little heat, the temperature often fell, to minus 40 Fahrenheit. Toilet facilities consisted of a dozen outhouses for several hundred men, who had to lineup in front of them in frigid January mornings. No provision had been made for recreation. Twice a day, the men were marched over a mile in the darkness to a converted warehouse on Portage Avenue where a catering firm provided what passed as breakfast and supper. The simple truth was that hardly anyone in Canada had a real knowledge of how a nation went about getting ready for a war.

One who thought he did know something, was Colonel Sam Hughes, Borden's Minister of Militia and National Defense.

Hughes an egotistical, eccentric and an abrasive man, became the most controversial figure in the Canadian war effort.

Within a few weeks of the outbreak of the war, Hughes had organized and set in operation a training camp and staging area for Canadian troops in Val Cartier, not far from

Quebec City. He was personally in command and on October 14 having seen 'his boys' off, hurried ahead of them in a fast ocean liner. Arriving in London, Hughes was told the British Office under the command of Lord Kitchener planned to break up the Canadian recruits and place the men under the more experienced British officers.

Hughes protested.

"You have my orders. Carry the out!" Kitchener told Hughes, but Hughes replied with anger, "I'll be damned if I will!" and made his exit. Hughes won the battle for Canadian soldiers to fight as a unit.

While police were chasing aliens, Erin realized that she had become pregnant. One minute she was afraid, the next she wanted to be true. She went to see Dr. Kozak and he confirmed her suspicion assuring Erin that the child would be in perfect health and probably born in July. Erin was going to discuss the pregnancy and what Dr. Kozak had said with her aunt Patricia and Margaret but decided against it.

Sometimes Erin thought Pawlo should feel triumph, and then she thought he would be furious.

She toyed with the idea of giving up the child, once it was born, for adoption, but decided against that too. Finally Erin decided to hide her pregnancy as best she could, although this would be difficult as time went on, and her pupils would be suspicious and tell their parents that their teacher suddenly had a big tummy.

In her bedroom, Erin posed with her tummy pulling it though she was afraid it would hurt her child. Erin began wondering if the School Board would fire her, what the Church would say about a child born out of wedlock. Would there be a scandal because Catholic girls weren't supposed to have illegitimate children. Would her uncle and aunt kick her out? Erin was filled with pity until Patricia, who heard Erin in her room, knocked on the door, and seeing her niece upset, asked, "Erin, what is the matter?"

When Erin told Patricia about the pregnancy, the two women talked 'Women-talk.' Aunt Patricia was so kind and frank about Erin's pregnancy that the anxiety lapsed.
Erin had become not only an excellent teacher but also a loving companion.

Since coming to Canada, she became a poised, delightful person and developed qualities of leadership.

"What will you name the child?" Patricia asked.

"If it's a boy, I don't know, Paul, I guess."

"And if it's a girl?"

"I'll name her Patricia."

"That would be kind of you."

Erin was pleased the way Patricia felt and when she left the room. Erin prayed that God would be merciful about her unmarried status and understand that what had happened between her and Pawlo was an accident.

CHAPTER ELEVEN

Winnipeg – October, 1914

In the hysteria that followed the outbreak of the war, Ukrainians found themselves as Austrian aliens, hostile to the Allies and subjected to increased discriminatory treatment. Thousands were dismissed from their jobs and thousands more, rounded up and interned in twenty-four concentration camps from Prince Edward Island to British Columbia.

In the middle of the night during September, Pawlo and Petro were sleeping when there was a knock on the door of their living quarters above the Mancan Store.

"Who is it?" Paul asked in his underwear.

"Police," a voice answered.

For several seconds Pawlo thought Erin may be in trouble, but that was not the case. As soon as he opened the door, a policeman flashed a light on Pawlo's face, seized him and Petro, and declared Pawlo Bilyi and Petro Czorny, you are under arrest."

"You caught me with my pants down," Pawlo protested but a second policeman said," "We expect cooperation, so both of you get moving."

"What are we arrested for?" Petro asked in a frightened manner while clutching to a wrinkled registration card.

"Both of you have the misfortune to be citizens of the Austro-Hungarian Empire, an enemy of the British Empire."

"This must be a mistake?" Petro said believing in his own innocence.

Pawlo and Petro were accused of missing an appointment to report to the North West Mounted Police, like all enemy aliens were ordered to do once a week, although some employers agreed to cut the period down to once a month.

"Where are you taking us?" Pawlo continued as he and Petro were shoved into a paddy wagon.

Impatient, the second policeman said, "The Fort Gary detention camp is already filled so we are taking you to the Brandon Camp."

"We came to Canada in search of freedom and you are placing us into a prison. How come? And how about the Mancan Store and the corporation?" Pawlo continued.

"The store and Mancan will be confiscated," the first policeman answered, "Both of you are enemies. Can't you see? Canada is at war! Come on, let's go."

"Hey, you have no authority to confiscate the Mancan Store, but if you do, we want you to contact Dr. Kozak," Pawlo said and give police the address.

The period of World War 1 (1914 – 1918) was difficult on Ukrainian Canadians. Most of them arrived in Canada with Austrian passports and Austria/Hungry were allied with Germany against Britain, France and eventually United States.
Anglo Canadians did not generally understand that Ukrainians had belonged to a nationality that was held captive within the Austro-Hungarian Empire.

Ten-thousand Ukrainian Canadian males served in the Canadian Army during the war. In order to fight for Canada many anglicised their surnames to Smith and Jones. One however, who did not his change his name was a volunteer by the name Filip Konowal who for his exceptional courage and velour with the 47th Infantry Battalion of the Canadian Expeditionary Force in France, was awarded the Victoria Cross, the highest decoration of the British Empire.

Winnipeg – June 1915

By June 1915, just over 5000 persons were interned in Canadian concentration camps, and another 48,500 were paroled. About half of those interned were Ukrainians from the Austria-Hungarian occupied area of Galicia. Hundreds of other Ukrainians were fired or forced from their jobs for no particular reason. Some were physically assaulted, while others had their property vandalized and stolen. All Ukrainians that had arrived with Austrian passports were required to register as aliens. Their democratic rights were curtailed and all naturalization into Canadian citizenship ceased. The publication of Ukrainian newspapers was suspended at first and publishers were later ordered to print parallel versions, in Ukrainian and English.

A delegation of Anglo Canadians even petitioned the Manitoba legislature to intern and deport all Ukrainians. The basic premise of Canadian-British justice that a person is considered innocent until proven guilty did not apply to everyone.

Brandon, Manitoba – Concentration Camp # 10 – October, 1914

In a matter of hours Pawlo and Petro were taken to the Brandon Detention Camp, designated Military District #10, 175 miles west of Winnipeg where Major John Matheson and three lieutenants: D.V. Coleman, Frank Crean and S. Crosthwait, were in charge, It was Major Matheson who greeted Pawlo and Petro and said do them, "And don't try to escape or else you'll get shot."

The compound, a makeshift camp, included the old Wheat City Arena located on land fenced with barbed wire and not far from the Assiniboine River. The camp had its own rail siding, mess hall, kitchen, bakery, general store and warehouses.

There were 250 internees milling around when Pawlo and Petro arrived: Ukrainians, Poles, Germans, Croats, all with Austria-Hungarian Empire background and all powerless, wondering what to do. There was little hope when the same guard that admitted Pawlo and Petro said, "Both of you will occupy barrack number 10."

Pawlo and Petro soon realized that they were prisoners of war and were subjected to military drills, even if they weren't soldiers, and forced to clear forests and build roads.

Major-General William Otter, a career military man who fought in the Metis uprising of 1885 in Cut Knife, Saskatchewan and the Boer War in 1899, was in charge of the overall interment operations. Of the 8,800 internees in Canada Otter classified 3,138 as true prisoners of war, either men who were in the army reserve in their home countries or were captured carrying arms. Their meals were plain with plenty of water to wash down the food. They slept on the bare floor with only one blanket and when they could not sleep, they could not help but reflect on their past and future.

Most of the internees were single, unemployed men who posed little if any threat to national security. Their crime was that they were born of Austrian bondage and to have come from countries allied with Germany, which was at war with Britain. "How long is it going to last? What crimes have I committed against Canada? What if they decide to charge me with espionage? Why did I leave Galicia in the first place?"

These and other similar questions Pawlo and Petro asked themselves.

In the barracks, one day, there were internees who, like Pawlo and Petro, for lunch were served two slices of bread, a piece of meat, a leaf of raw cabbage and tea and sugar. Before lunch, Lieutenant Crosthwait appeared in the barracks doorway and hollered, "Any complaints?"

Everyone answered, "No."

Petro did too, but actually felt there were a lot of things to complain about.

"We shall find out what kind of justice they practice here when he asks the same question next time," Petro said to Pawlo who usually sat together.

Several days later, after lunch, instead of answering the usual, "No," Petro answered back, "Yes, I do have a complaint."

The German internees who received better care than the Ukrainians and were excepted from the worst of the work, while sitting next to Petro, were dismayed and one even found the gumption to say to him, "Shut up," and another, "Oh, no. You'll get us into more trouble."

Lieutenant Crosthwait looked around, and seeing everyone seated but Petro, said, "What's your complaint?"

"I want more food to eat."
German inmates immediately got after Petro
to keep quiet and not to make further demands
for fear that even the small amount of food
they were getting would be cut and all the
inmates end up fasting.
Petro's protest was ignored and he was dared
to complain again.

Each day the prisoner's life was monotonous.
They were however, allowed time for a walk
in the courtyard that was encoded with a
barbed wire fence and guarded by soldiers
with bayonets fixed to their rifles.
Among the inmates was a German who did
not care about walking. Instead he often stood
by the fence and talked to himself. One day,
Petro approached the German and said to him,
"Didn't I meet you on a train from Quebec
City to Winnipeg?"
"You may have. Aren't you the one playing
cards with two Irish school teachers and I
asked you while we passed through Northern
Ontario wilderness, why you weren't crying
like the rest of us?" the German asked.

After Petro recalled the incident his reply was, "I remember, you are Hans Gruber, and you said at the time what was worse than living in the Austro-Hungarian Empire was to be employed by an Englishman in Winnipeg. Now I believe it."

Petro and Gruber talked for a short while and then went their separate ways, but not before they agreed to meet again.

The inmates were confined to their barracks and cut off from rest of the world during the first six weeks. Reading material was strictly censored. Later they still led an animal-like existence completely ignorant of what went on in the world outside, some sick, some despondent, some trying to escape and some even committing suicide.

One day a trainload of prisoners arrived at the camp and were surrounded by inmates who bombarded them with questions, "Where were you captured?" "Where did you come from?" "How is the war progressing?" "Is it true the Russians and Austrians have been driven out of Poland?"

Towards evening, the barracks were swarmed with other men returning from work.

Then came the call for supper that consisted
of a spoonful of sauerkraut and a potato
served on a tin plate, and tea served in a tin
cup. There was plenty of bread and a gallon of
plum jam to go with it. On the jam can were
the words, "Distributed by Windsor Co. Ltd.
After supper the barracks hummed with
conversation until 9:00 p. m. Then came a
curfew, and everyone went off to sleep. The
internees' rose at 7:00 a. m. and after
breakfast rose to their feet into two files.
Major Matheson called out a number and the
inmate hearing it, answered, "Yes."
Several inmates who at one time belonged to
the reserve army in Austria, answered with a,
"Here."
Everyone stood at attention, although camp
regulations did not call for it.
"That type of a response comes from a slave,"
Petro said to another inmate.
Within an hour, the inmates were all outside
doing something. Mostly it was at road
construction. Pawlo and Petro were supplied
with long-handled shovels and led at gunpoint
towards a large building, which was built out
of massive timbers, and guards were stationed
around it. Pawlo and Petro speculated the
building was the camp jail where inmates
were abused by jail guards.

Nearby internees worked on road construction and dug ditches on each side of a strip of land cleared for construction of a highway. Pawlo and Petro dug ditches on each side of the strip and pitched the earth onto the middle.

"Such is the exploitation of manpower in a forced labor camp," Petro said to Pawlo and he agreed with that assessment.

"Had I cheated someone or stolen from someone, then I could understand. Why should we work at the point of a bayonet for a spoonful of jam? Especially, when the jam is distributed by the Windsor Company Ltd. in Winnipeg."

There were fifty inmates on this particular project where a civilian was a foreman. When the foreman noticed Petro working lazily, he strode up to him and enquired angrily, "Why are you standing around and not working?"

'Big shot", Petro thought but answered, "What right have you got to threaten me?" Those were among the first English words Petro picked up in the English language as a university student in Lvov.

The foreman's face turned as red as a beet, his eyeballs were as large as a hen's egg and ordered a soldier standing next to him to incarcerate Petro into jail. The soldier handcuffed Petro and said, "Follow me, Bohunk."

The soldier and Petro hadn't walked more than fifty steps when they heard voices behind them, "Hey, let's go too."

Turning around Petro saw men who worked with him had dropped their spades and shovels and were following him and the soldier,

"What a wonderful feeling to see that they too understand what freedom means," Petro said to the soldier.

It didn't seem like a long walk as the soldier incarcerated Petro. As soon as this was done, the inmates that followed headed for the barracks instead of returning to work. Meanwhile, Petro, once he was in jail kept thinking of Margaret and thought, "A prison is a prison no matter where."

All sorts of thoughts ran through Petro's mind while he was in solitary confinement, some of them were disturbing. Not only did he think of Margaret but also the sad commentary on a system that used jails to drive fear into the hearts of innocent people and subject them to forced labor.

Petro thought, "What good will it do to rebel? It is wartime. I have no rights in Canada. Instead of protesting would it not be better to resort to subterfuge and deceit?"

Next morning, guards unbolted the jail door and with bayonets by their sides, took Petro to the courtroom. Behind the table sat the entire tribunal including Major Matheson and Lieutenant Croswaith. On Petro's left was an interpreter to make certain Petro understood each word. On his right, stood a soldier guard holding a rifle.

In addition to regular questions pertaining to his identification, Major Matheson asked, "Petro Czorny, why have you refused to work?"

Petro put on his bold front and in an aggressive manner answered, "From childhood until yesterday I had never held a shovel in my hands and I do not know how to work with one."

As the interpreter translated the answer into English Major Matheson raised his eyebrows and continued, "What kind of work do you normally do?"

Petro put on a more imposing front, "I worked on a large plantation of poppies near Lvov and a rope factory, which used hemp. Now I'm an entrepreneur and have farming and corporate experience."

"What made you come to Canada?" Major Matheson continued questioning.

"Aside from farming I came to Canada to do research if opium in poppy seed makes soldiers fall asleep, and if hemp is a fibre strong enough to make parachutes for Canadian soldiers fighting in France."

Who could tell Petro was lying? And if he was questioned further about poppies and hemp Petro could say that he and Mancan were conducting scientific research work. At any rate Petro noticed that from time to time Major Matheson glanced in a friendly way, as though he believed Petro. The Major and Petro exchanged additional dialogue until the interpreter said to Petro and explained the decision of the court.

"Instead of working on road construction, from now on, you are to pick up litter and papers around the barracks. That's your new job."

As Petro walked out the courtroom, he could hardly keep from smiling. "It's a wonder I wasn't commissioned to grow poppies and hemp in the concentration camp," he said to the interpreter.

It helped Petro to get out of tasks other internees were required to perform. He would not touch another shovel, spade or axe.

Where was he going to look for litter?

Most likely near the barbed wire fence.

Before long, everything would be covered with snow three-feet deep.

Before Christmas came Petro vowed that he would escape.

CHAPTER 7

Brandon, Manitoba - Concentration Camp # 10 - November, 1914

It was a cold November day in 1914 as Pawlo and Petro were peering through the barbed wire fence, that they noticed two women approaching the concentration camp. As the distance got shorter they were delighted the women turned out to be Erin and Margaret Carpenter.

Once inside the camp's main office, Major Crosthwait permitted Pawlo, Petro, Erin and Margaret to speak to each other. "For thirty minutes only and you will have to leave," the Major said to Erin and brought the two couples into a vacant room.

There was a moment of sadness but some happiness too, when Erin said to Pawlo, "The Mancan Corporation and its downtown store had not been confiscated and under the supervision of Dr. Kozak. "The staff you and Petro trained is able to carry on without you."

"Good, good, good," Pawlo said.

"And do you want to know something else?" Next, Erin surprised Pawlo when she said, "Dr. Kozak confirms that I'm going to have a baby."

What Margaret and Petro talked about next, is still not known except that their hearts swelled with love they felt for each other. When they changed to another topic Margaret asked Petro, "How are they treating you here?"

"No human eye should see some of the things the guards to prisoners."

"Tell me about it."

"Well, if I must. Last night the guards strung me up to the ceiling upside down and forced me to drink my own urine. Inmates are beaten and some hung by their wrists."

"How awful. The guards do that because you are Ukrainian?"

"And, that I'm an enemy of Canada."

"Some say it's the Catholic Bishop Budka's fault," Pawlo cut in. "Because he urged us to enlist in the Austrian army."

"Then why isn't Bishop Budka interned?" Erin asked.

"Good question. Maybe the Bishop doesn't know how to use a spade, shovel or an axe."

"Or work in the coal mines, build highways, clear timber, or pick up leaves in parks, which prisoners are doing," Margaret continued.

"Then how about Ivan Kazakoff? How come he's not interned?" Erin went on.

"Because he isn't Ukrainian."

"What is he then?"

"He's Russian."

Thirty minutes later, the guard on duty told Margaret and Erin that it was time to leave, and they did sadly, but not before each had planted a kiss on their respected friend's cheeks and then their lips.

Erin and Margaret visited Pawlo and Petro as often as they could and kept them abreast of what was taking place in the world of Mancan. In between visits, they exchanged letters. In one letter Petro wrote to Margaret, "Living conditions here are primitive. Prisoners are subjected each day to ten hours of hard labor and suffer from hunger, depression and beatings even when men faint they are ordered to work."

In his letter to Erin Pawlo wrote, "There are men trying to escape every day because living conditions are very poor, so that we can't go on much longer. We are not getting enough food. We are hungry as dogs. Prisoners know nothing about the war because most of them are peasants and illiterate.

They came to Canada to escape military service but ended up behind barbed wire. We have no recourse to the courts or to legal counsel."

In another letter, Erin and Margaret suggested Pawlo and Petro Anglicize their names from Pawlo Bilyi to Paul White and Petro Czorny to Peter Black, which translated from Ukrainian to English, the names meant.

In a joint letter Pawlo and Petro responded with, "We have decided to change our names to Black and White but on condition that you marry us as soon as we are set free."

In another letter, Erin wrote that it was now risky for non-Anglophones to walk in downtown Winnipeg without proper identification and no one would listen to voices of harassment or allegations that Ukrainians belonged to an organization designated to be subversive.

Brandon Concentration Camp # 10 – December, 1914

On a December cold morning, Pawlo found Margaret's letter to Petro unopened and Petro missing.

When Pawlo approached a guard and enquired about his partner the guard replied in a cold manner, "Petro Czorny has escaped."

In a predominantly Ukrainian camp population of 800, there were escape attempts before.

Tunneling and jumping out a window were a favorite method. Some were shot to death trying to escape and several more wounded in attempts.

Petro's escape took place after he struck a friendly relationship with the German inmate Hans Gruber. Petro had met Gruber earlier while on a train between Quebec City and Winnipeg and more recently in the concentration camp that both aliens were incarcerated in.

On the night of the escape a freak snowstorm swept across southern Manitoba bringing an unexpected White Christmas after a wreaking havoc on the Canadian prairie.

Despite temperatures that reached 40 degrees below Fahrenheit, and winds gusting as high as 80 miles an hour, Petro and Gruber jumped out a barracks window and raced as fast as their legs could carry them. As they ran in pitch-darkness, a guard on duty spotted shadowy figures and shouted, "Halt!"

Petro and Gruber did not stop running. The guard fired a shot but did not hit anyone. The second shot did. The bullet struck Gruber and minutes later he lay in a snow bank, dead. Petro was fortunate.

Not only did another bullet miss him but also the drifting snow, covered his tracks. During the blizzard Petro climbed an embankment and ran as fast as he could.

Probably a guardian angel was guiding Petro because he ran in the dead of the night darkness over snow-covered ditches, moles and rocks until he came to a cabin situated near a railway. As Petro approached the cabin he saw a shining light and through a window a middle-aged couple that had just come home from what seemed to be a happy occasion.

Petro knocked on the door and when it opened, said to the lady of the house, "I realize it's late at night and I'm a stranger but I seem to be lost. I won't take up much of your time but may I please come inside and warm up?"

After seeing Petro shivering and with frozen cheeks and ears, introductions were exchanged, and Petro invited inside, where the lady of the house said, "If you were in the cold much longer you'd catch pneumonia. Your outer clothing needs drying."

An aroma of Christmas baking permeated the cabin. There were neither glittering lights nor colored tinsel to sparkle and glisten the Christmas tree placed in one corner of the cabin.

The tree was decorated with candles, candy canes, oranges and apples and small ornaments. And although there were no children's stockings hanging from the mantle Christmas had not lost its meaning for the cabin occupants Carl and Mary Olsen – they were not only returning home from celebrating the birth of Jesus by attending a midnight church service in Brandon but also their first wedding anniversary.

Although the decorations on the Christmas tree did not sparkle and there were no children, there was an open fireplace with crackling logs, the flames roaring up the chimney, defying Jack Frost.

With Carl's help, Petro stripped down to his underwear but there wasn't much of Petro as he was lean, almost ghostly in appearance and it seemed as if he had not eaten in weeks. In his long john's Petro looked like a young son that any mother would love to cuddle. Seeing the condition Petro was in, Mary said in jest that she had seen bigger bones on a turkey she had prepared for the Christmas dinner, but his long narrow face with sunken cheeks and pale fast-moving eyes was the face of a man with determination and unconquerable will.

When Petro handed his clothes to Mary to hang on a chair near the fireplace, Petro appeared lost so she said to him, "Would you like something to eat?"
"That would be kind of you."
While handing him a robe Mary said, "Here, you can put Carl's robe on while your clothes dry out. I'll prepare you a turkey dinner as quickly as I can."
When this was done, Carl said to Petro, "How about joining Mary and me in a Christmas drink while your clothes are drying?"
Without waiting for a reply Mary broke in, "An excellent idea."

Carl then placed a bottle in the middle of the kitchen table, poured its contents into glasses and handed one to Petro who took a mouthful. It was several seconds before Petro could get his breath back. "This is powerful stuff. What is it?" he said.

"Pure alcohol, right out of the spout, double distilled," Carl replied and went on, lowering his gravelly voice, "If Sam Bronfman in Saskatchewan can do it, why can't I?"

There was something about Petro that the drink did to him. It made him relax and temporarily forget his escape from the concentration camp and asked Carl and Mary how they met.

"Through *Heads and Hands*. It's a magazine published in New York, especially for the lovelorn," Carl said.

"You met through a magazine advertisement?"

"We did," Mary replied, filled her glass again and then showed Petro a copy of the magazine. It was full of pictures, advertisements and testimonials from people who got married through it and were happy.

"We are one of those couples," Carl said. "I sent a letter to the magazine saying that I was honest, dependable, a farmer and looking for a wife. My advert said, Object Matrimony. No triflers please."

Petro wanted to know more.

"When I saw the advert I enclosed a snapshot, wrote Carl a letter and waited for the next move." Mary answered.

And then Carl took over, "Within two weeks I had five replies I guess not many city women want to marry farmers these days, but I guess Mary, did."

"And then what happened?"

"Well, I read each letter, but the one I enjoyed the most along with the photograph was Mary's. She sounded like a sensible girl and although no spring chicken or flower in bloom, she could spell words correctly so that she must be educated."

"It was like choosing a coyote rifle from Eaton's catalogue," Mary continued. "But when Carl showed some interest we exchanged more letters during the summer. I finally decided I wanted to see my future husband for myself so I came to Brandon."

"She looked me over and I looked her over. Although she was an American from Chicago and not a Canadian did not matter.

What did was that we were in love with each other. ``

Another hour passed, and then another, when Carl said to Petro, "Let's have another drink."

"Okay, but it will be my last, as my clothes are dry now."

"And then what happened?" Petro probed.

"Immediately Carl began calling me 'My Bride' and on Christmas Eve a year ago, he changed to a new pair of overalls, asked me to get dressed in my Sunday best, and we drove to the preacher's manse in a cutter and horse and got married." Mary said.

Carl gave Mary a peck on the cheek as she continued, "And this has been a year of bliss for both of us."

"It was the quickest shotgun marriage in Brandon," Carl said with a hearty laugh.

"So you have just returned from attending a Christmas midnight service when I startled you?" Petro apologized.

"That's all right. We went to the service with another couple that is celebrating their first anniversary also. Only Richard and Vera Nantong used the *Family Herald* before they decided to get married. Vera is originally from North Dakota." Mary said.

When Petro changed to his original clothing, he said to the recently married couple, "I hope your marriage works out. Both of you appear to be hard working people. I would enjoy spending more time with you but I'm afraid I must move on."

Carl glanced at his pocket watch. It was 6:30 a. m.

"Before you leave we want you to take home for your family a loaf of Christmas bread I baked," Mary said, tired and ready to go to bed.

"Family?" Petro thought as Margaret flashed through his mind. At first he was reluctant to accept the loaf, which had raisins in it, but when Carl assured him it was the best bread he had ever tasted, "Even better tasting than my mother used to bake." Petro accepted the loaf and stuffed it under his sheepskin coat. As Petro opened the door, which had a cedar bough with bells attached to it, Petro shook Carl and Mary's hands and wished each a, "Marry Christmas."

"And peace on earth. Goodwill to men." Mary said.

"Merry Christmas," Carl said again, and finally Petro made his exit.

By now the snowstorm had subsided substantially, but it was still bitterly cold. As Petro was walking, not knowing where he was, and footsteps echoing in the virgin snow, he heard a rooster crow. Soon the sun appeared on the horizon. To Petro it seemed as if the entire world was singing sheer joy, "Merry Christmas, Petro."

Hope is often elusive in a world prone to chaos and evil, and yet, it was as if in the days of the Bible two millennia ago when Jesus Christ offered comfort to the needy and the suffering. Every so often Petro stopped to catch his breath and the last time that he did, he heard church bells ringing in the distance. As he was listening to the bells he said to himself, "Now that the sun is rising I know my bearings."

Pointing southward Petro said, "That must be towards the American border."

An hour later, Petro reached a railroad and then heard the sound of a locomotive coming. It seemed close. "This could be a Christmas present I shall never forget," Petro thought as the train blew its whistle while coming around the bend and then he said, "I'll have to try and climb on board."

Hope gave way to strength and as the train was passing him, Petro grabbed on to the rear empty boxcar, climbed inside and stayed there until the train reached Minneapolis. The freight yard was near the passenger section and café where an elderly woman saw Petro get off, strolled towards him and said, "Merry Christmas sir. I don't know if you realize it but you have frozen ears."

"If that's the case it's not much of Christmas, is it?" Petro replied.

"Look. Now they are thawing and dropping discharge on your shoulder," the elderly woman, dressed in a black dress and a fur coat, said,

Petro was in a dilemma. He did not know what to do or say. He had no money and the loaf of bread Carl and Mary Olson had given him he had already eaten.

The elderly woman whose wrinkled face and drooping form told a story of hardship, felt sorry for Petro's plight, and took out a piece of cloth from her purse and tried to bandage Petro's ears. In the process she spoke sympathetically, so gently, that she reminded Petro of his own mother.

"What's your name?" the elderly woman asked and Petro replied, "My name is Petro Czorny."

"And where are you going?"

Petro did not want to tell the elderly woman that he had escaped from the Brandon Concentration Camp so he pretended he did not hear her. "The old woman must be a detective," he thought.

Besides the pain in his ears lobes Petro also felt pans of hunger so the elderly woman bought him several chocolate bars and insisted knowing where he was going.
Petro did not know himself so he said.
"Chicago."
The more Petro thought about it, the more he wanted to go to Chicago. He had heard about Chicago from Nathan Tarnoff when he and Pawlo purchased the Tarnoff General Store in the north-end of Winnipeg and more recently Mary Olson, who dried his clothing, came from Chicago.
The elderly woman said, "I'm going to Chicago too. As a matter of fact, the train will be leaving shortly. Will you accompany me?"
Not quite sure that he understood her, the elderly woman showed Petro a train ticket stamped Chicago, went to the ticket agent and purchased one for Petro also.
"I won't be able to pay you back." Petro said.
"The good Lord willing you may be able someday. If I were you I wouldn't worry."
"I'm very grateful for your kindness," Petro said as nearby, at the passenger train station, in the hustle and bustle of a Christmas day, a conductor could be heard calling, "All aboard for Chicago!"

Petro felt uncomfortable about the strange woman's concern for him. But at the same time thankful for her help at a time of need. Aboard the passenger train the elderly woman took a seat next to a window and motioned for Petro suggesting that he sit next to her.

"I can't refuse," Petro thought, "What shall I do if I can't shake her off?"

Rocked by the train, Petro soon felt drowsy. He yawned. How he hoped for some sleep after riding in the empty and cold boxcar. But besides this elderly woman? Maybe if she was much younger, prettier and her voice stronger.

Before Petro figured out what to do, he was sleeping next to her. On awakening Petro felt embarrassed because his head was resting on the elderly woman's breasts. Bewildered Petro looked around him. Saw some passengers smiling. Petro knew the predicament he was in, so apologized to the elderly woman profusely.

"Oh, that's nothing to worry about," she assured him. "When you fell asleep your head was hanging over the armrest.

It must have been uncomfortable so I moved
it and placed it on my chest,"
A tear glistened in the elderly woman's eyes.
Petro noticed it and feeling more at ease
began openly to talk to her.
"My husband and I once had a son who
reminds me of you but Abraham died
recently," the elderly woman said as tears
began to fill her eyes.
"Don't cry," Petro said softly. "I once had a
mother as loving and kind as you and she died
too,"
While both tried to suppress their tears, Petro
excused himself and went to the washroom.
Looking into a mirror he cried out, "This
can't be me, Petro Czorny!"
The sight in the mirror reminded Petro that his
ears looked like marinated herrings his father
use to buy at Christmas time. The sight was
repulsive. When Petro washed up he stood
for a moment looking at himself in the mirror
again and couldn't believe how his looks
improved. "That's better." he said.
As soon as Petro returned to his seat his
benefactor complimented him on his new
appearance and asked many questions, the
first was, "What are you going to do in
Chicago?"
"I'm not certain."

"Are you married?'

"No. I live alone and have no family."

"Where are you going to live while in Chicago?'

Petro shrugged his shoulders, "I'm not certain."

"You aren't certain about many things young man," the elderly woman said and went on, "Do you know anyone in Chicago?"

Petro assured her that he knew a Jew by the name of Nathan Tarnoff who once lived in Winnipeg.

"Son, you want to know something?" the elderly woman said.

Intrigued, Petro said, "What?"

"Did I hear you correctly? You did say his name was Nathan Tarnoff and that he once lived in Winnipeg?"

"That's correct. We became friends."

"Do you want to know something else?"

"For the second time Petro said, "What?"

"I'm his wife, Hadassah. Why don't you come and live with us. Perhaps my husband could use extra help in the furniture store we own."

"Want to know something," Petro said.

This time it was Mrs. Tarnoff's turn to say, "What?"

"If your husband is as kind as you are, I know he'll find work for me despite my herring-like ears. Merry Christmas. Mrs. Tarnoff."
"Being Jewish we do not celebrate Christmas like you do," Mrs. Tarnoff said. "But at any rate, Merry Christmas, many of them."

Mrs. Tarnoff picked up a copy of the *Tribune* from a newspaper vendor and then both climbed into a taxi and Mrs. Tranoff read an article about President Wilson who stated: "This is a peace loving nation. Everything we hold dear depends on peace."
President Wilson was making efforts to bring cessation to the war and suggested, "Peace without victory" but the offer was scorned by Germany.
On another page of the Tribune the headline read: Women from Los Angeles to Cape Cod Are Singing "I Don't Want My Son to Be a Soldier."

CHAPTER TWELVE

Chicago - 1915

Petro lived with the Turnoff's and worked in their furniture store in Chicago from the latter part of December until May 1915. In that time he attended a jazz concert by Paul Whitman and on the radio heard Jess Willard knockout the heavyweight-boxing champion, Jack Johnson, after twenty rounds in a bout in Havana, thus winning the title. Petro also heard the news that St. Louis Cardinals bought second baseman, Roger Hornsby, for $400 and who became one of the greatest players of the game and seven times the National Baseball League batting champion. Petro was also earning money, not as much as Hornsby made but enough for a ticket that would take him to London.

As soon as he had enough money saved and before his ears healed, Petro traveled to New York where he purchased a ticket and boarded a Cunard Line luxury ship, Lusitanian, bound from New York to Liverpool. Petro had never seen such a large ship and only read about the Titanic it sank off the coast of Newfoundland.

Petro was awed by the ship's spaciousness compared to the S. S. Christiana that brought him from Liverpool to Canada.

While onboard. Petro struck up conversations with Americans Alfred Gwynne Vanderbilt, playwright Charles and theatrical producer Charles Frochman, but not necessarily in that order. Petro was in conversation with Vanderbilt about the Austrian and German steamships that were interned in American ports when a dramatic thing happened – the Lusitania was struck by a German U-20 torpedo and began sinking. The date was May 7, 1915. Time 2:10 p. m. Location: twelve miles off Old Head of Kinsale, southern Ireland.

The torpedo struck the starboard side directly behind the bridge. There was a tremendous explosion and the liner listed fifteen degrees. Then there was a second explosion, louder than the first. The bridge was demolished and the Lusitania stopped dead, the stern out of water.

Slowly the Lusitania began to nose under the starboard and absolute panic reigned.

Many of the 26 collapsible canvass lifeboats
stored between the 22, two and one-half ton
wooden boats, could not be lowered; both
collapsible boats and passengers were crushed
against the hull.

On the port side however, where Petro was
standing, lifeboats that were available plunged
into the sea.
By now the German torpedo, which had
pierced the coalbunkers ignited the fuel and
set off the contraband cargo. It was the second
explosion that sank the Lusitania.
Within 18 minutes the luxury liner was
floating on the ocean's surface. One of those
in a floating lifeboat was Petro Czorny.
In the end there was a loss of 1198 lives but
Petro was fortunate as he managed to reach
the shore of Ireland safely. A destroyer sent
out to search for survivors from the nearby
Royal Navy base Cobh picked up his lifeboat.

Cobh, Ireland – May 18, 1915

Petro saw Cobh as an attractive hilly town
dominated by its 19th century cathedral, St.
Colman's that had an elegant spire.

It was during a routine medical checkup that Petro said to the doctor examining him, "How far is Cork from Cobh?"

"Fifteen miles," the doctor replied placing his stethoscope to one side.

"And what is the best way to get there?"

"By train. There's regular service from Kent station on Lower Glenmire Road."

As soon as Petro's examination was over and was told that he was in excellent health and free to continue his journey, Petro walked to Kent station and purchased a ticket to Cork. The train journey gave Petro a commanding view of the harbor. A passenger seated next to him said when Blackrock Castle came into view, "William Penn, the founder of the Pennsylvania colony was born in Cork and it's believed he stayed in the castle before sailing to America."

except that it invaded Canada in 1812, and Canada had won the war.

"William Penn? He was a Quaker and only one of thousands who had sailed from Cork hoping for a better life in the New World."

As soon as the train reached Cork, Petro got off and said he wasn't familiar with American history and walked towards the main business and shopping centre, which lay on an island created by two channels of the River Lee.

When Petro reached Patricia Street, Cork's most famous statue that of Father Theobald Mathew (1790 -1861), was staring at him. On the statue base there was printing that said Father Mathew led a nation-wide temperance crusade, no small feat in a country as for of its pints as this one. In the first year of his campaign Father Mathew enrolled a startling 150,000 people, with the movement, later spreading to Scotland, England, America and Canada.

It was here that Petro took his bearings and the thing on his mind was to find lodging for the night and locate Margaret's parents, Sean and Anne Carpenter, who operated a small clothing store on the ground floor, with living quarters on top on Davis Street.

Petro bought a map and a newspaper and sat down to study them as a passerby glanced at him. Petro simply dressed as he had lost all of his belongings when the Lusitania sank. He knew he had to find a room before nightfall. The question was where to start.

He picked out two addresses and asked the
passerby which of the two hotels he would
recommend.

"I would choose Jury's Hotel on Western
Road. It's a five minute walk from here, next
to the river and has an excellent bar," the
passerby said.

"Thank you, sir."

Then the passerby asked, "Where are you
from?"

"Canada."

Petro felt sad as he said Canada. It seemed
like days since he escaped from the Brandon
Concentration Camp as an enemy of the
country.

"Going to live here?"

"No. I'm on my way to London but first I
must find the Carpenters who live on Davis
Street."

Petro walked to the hotel and registered. He
counted his dwindling money nervously and
sat on a bed that had a crucifix over the bed
and two colored landscapes by unknown Irish
artists. By now it was eleven o'clock and
Petro did not want to disturb the Carpenters.
Instead he went downstairs to a bar, ordered a
pint of beer and sat down. For Petro the Cork
accent took some getting used to.

He soon discovered the communication problem was not confined to visitors from overseas and that even Dubliners found Corkorians incomprehensible at times and vice versa. But after an hour Petro became attuned to the Cork lilt and often found himself picking up certain intonations.

Petro enjoyed the Irish hospitality, which seemed talking and drinking was a past time. Naturally, everyone talked about the sinking of the Lusitania but Petro did not let on that he was one of the survivors. During the course of conversation with Irishmen, Petro discovered that in Ireland the principal social institution, after the Church and home, was the pub. He also discovered that the Cork man owns a patented cutting humor and a natural distaste for Dublin or anything else non-Cork.

Before Petro retired for the night he joined others in singing the song 'On the Banks of My Own Lovely Lee' that nearly brought tears to his eyes. As he drifted to sleep, Petro knew he would never forget the City of Cork.

The following day, Petro met Sean and Anne Carpenter shortly before noon at the clothing store they owned.

He received a warm, if somewhat inquisitive welcome. Sean Carpenter was a sportsman. His hurling team was a perennial power. He played and bet on, anything that ran or any spheroid that is batted, kicked or flung. Sean Carpenter was the most generous supporter of the country's largest greyhound track and above all, a Republican.

The Carpenters had heard a lot about Petro Czorny through letters that they received from Margaret.

"And how is Margaret doing now that she's blind?" Anne asked to which Petro replied, "When I saw her last she was writing fiction about the immigrant Ukrainian women."

"And Erin?"

"Erin is doing splendidly as far as I know. Her boyfriend, Pawlo Bilyi however, is still incarcerated in the Brandon German Concentration Camp."

For the next while the Carpenter's and Petro talked about Margaret, Erin, Pawlo and Petro, the Brandon Concentration Camp that he escaped and the sinking of the Lusitania.

Sean said. "You are fortunate to be alive."

"I am, indeed."

The conversation continued for another hour when the Carpenter's invited Petro for dinner, to stay overnight and explore the city.

"I would be delighted to spend the night at your residence," Petro said and when dinner time came, Anne Carpenter's idea of a good meal wasn't boiled meant with lots of boiled vegetables but pickled pigs' trotters and colcannon, a potato cake with cream poured over it. Colcannon was served with a ring, a thimble, a button and a sixpence concealed inside.

While eating Petro found the ring to which Anne responded with, "You'll get married, remain a bachelor or become rich."

"Perhaps it will be Margaret. She thinks a lot of you," Sean said.

"To be candid, the thought has crossed my mind."

"Good. Anne and I will be looking forward to dance on Margaret's and your wedding day."

"It depends on the war," Petro said and left it at that.

After they had eaten, and everyone made themselves comfortable in the living room, Anne said, "Let's telephone Margaret and Erin in Canada."

Petro looked nervously at Anne and wondered if she could have read his mind. Now that he was on the other side of the Atlantic the North West Mounted Police wouldn't care to find and incarcerate him.

When the long distance operator put the call through Anne said, "Here Petro, surprise Margaret."

Petro picked up the receiver and said, "Margaret, do you know who is speaking?"

"It's you sweetheart, Petro. I was wondering if you would ever write or call. How are you doing?"

"Fine, thank you. And you?"

"I'm fine too."

"Do you know where I'm calling from?"

"It certainly isn't from the Brandon Concentration Camp. Is it?"

"From your Mom and Dad's place, in Cork, Ireland. And I promise you one thing."

"What?"

"You'll never find me in a Canadian concentration camp again."

As the conversation continued Petro told Margaret all there was to know about his escape and the sinking of the Lusitania.

"And what's next?" Margaret kept probing.

"I'll be leaving tomorrow for London."

"London? What on earth for?"

"To enlist with the Royal Air Corps."

Petro and Margaret talked for ten minutes. After speaking to Erin the senior Carpenter's took over.

In their segment of conversation Petro and Margaret spoke with detached clarity and promised that they would be true to each other. Now that he had met Margaret's parents he seemed much closer to her. That night before falling asleep, Petro wrote Margaret a letter saying he would see her as soon as the war was over.

The letter ended with a P. S.

"And when the war is over we'll get married. Lots of love.

Peter Black, alias Petro Czorny.

London – May 20, 1915

The following day it was foggy outside and exactly ten minutes past four in the afternoon when Petro was at the Royal Air Corps Recruiting Theatre in London. As he entered the building he heard a BBC announcer say that Allied forces were having a difficult time in France against the Germans.

How strange life was. Petro was in London instead of Winnipeg, wondering when the war would end, if it would, and how he could help personally. As Petro approached the receptionist she politely said to him, "May I help you?"

"Please. I would like to speak to a recruiting officer."

"Certainly, one will be with you shortly. Please be seated."

Minutes later, a recruiting officer appeared and introduced himself as, Corporal James Davis."

"Corporal, I would like to enlist in the Royal Air Corps." Petro said and was led to an office where the corporal sat behind a desk, picked up an application form and a pen. The first question on the application form was: Name?

'Peter Black," Petro replied.

The second question was: Address?

"Winnipeg, Canada," Petro replied.

"A Canadian?" Corporal Davis asked.

"Not yet," Petro replied and then in full detail explained his background and that fact he was Petro Czorny, had escaped from the Brandon detention camp and was a survivor of the Lusitania.

In the end, when the application form was completed and Peter Black was told by a medical examining officer that he was in excellent health, he reported for basic training and as his instructor put it, "Learn to fly the aeroplane, the latest innovation in warfare."

Ypres France – April, 1915

While Peter Black was riding out the drama of the sinking of the Lusitania and then enlisting in the Royal Air Corps, and even greater drama was taking place by a cast of Canadian volunteer soldiers in Europe in the trenches.

The Third Infantry Brigade commanded by Henry Crerar, which James Buller was a member, unleashed repeated attacks, but the Germans used chlorine gas.

The gas came across low-lying fields as drifting fog that soldiers saw as gray, some yellow and some green. When the gas struck the Algerian conscripts on the left of the Allied line they dropped their guns and ran as fast as their legs could carry them. Some civilians followed. All around scenes were apocalyptic.

A group of stragglers sobbed as they streamed through St. Julien, and James Buller, who had not yet seen or tasted the gas, reported in bewilderment to his headquarters, "The streets are full of running Niggers."

In the ensuing battle, less than twelve hours after the Canadian soldiers were aware of the gas, they experienced more trouble: the Ross Rifle they were using began to jam.
Without warning hundreds of Canadian soldiers began to weep, curse and pray in the face of advancing German troops while Canadian soldiers attempted to prey loose their jammed rifle bolts with trench shovels or heels of their army boots.
The gas too, proved more damaging than first expected. On the first day of the attack its power to destroy the human body had been established. It could destroy the human will and on the last minute of the exposure James Buller lost his desire to live. Buller was a victim of the Battle of Ypres and like 5,500 Canadian soldiers who were casualties in the battle his last words on earth were, "Go away, and let me die."

James Buller had not even had an opportunity to mail a letter he had written to Erin saying he would convert to Catholicism if necessary, as soon as the war was over. The letter was stuffed in his shirt pocket and dated April 23, 1915 when another soldier found and read the letter, as it was unsealed. Buller's letter said seldom have human beings ever had to exist under more appalling conditions that those endured by soldiers who moved to the front lines. There of course, was fear, although it was numbed after a time by boredom and fatigue and a sense of loneliness and hopelessness.

Buller in his letter to Erin wrote about moans and screams of the wounded, the horror of seeing friends maimed, blinded, turned into corpses. There was the general insanity of it all, and the particular reality of shell shock, the chronic concussion caused by the big guns that destroyed men's minds and the will to live.

Buller's letter continued: "But the worse even then the partial or whole death is the wretchedness of life in such circumstances.

We are forced to grovel in earth like animals; the men are wet, dirty and cold. Boots and uniforms mildew and fall apart. A soldier with a clean pair of socks to wear is envied.

Rotting of flesh between and around the toes is common. So is trench mouth. There are smells of sweat cordite and urine and fear of death. Rats as large as alley cats run through the trenches and grow slick and fat on putrefaction. And always there is the mud to contend with. Soldiers' sleep where and when they can. The meals are monotonous providing minimal sustenance and no uplifting spirits…"

When he soldier finished reading the letter he said to himself, "Yes, these are the conditions we fight in."

He didn't want Erin to hear about the horrifying truth and instead of mailing the letter dug a hole in the ground and buried it. Next day the soldier, like James Buller, had died.

Winnipeg – July 1915

It was July 15, 1915 when school was out for summer vacation that Erin gave birth to a baby girl, which she immediately named Patricia but did not have her baptized. During the next week a stream of visitors came to visit Erin and Little Patricia, as the visitors nicknamed her, with present and made quite a fuss about the child.

The senior Windsor admired the child too and said he would take for walks when she got older, "And when she gets older still I'll take her to Ottawa and watch me in the House of Commons. Never can tell Patricia my someday become Canada's first woman prime minister."

Windsor was proud of Little Patricia because he, after having John, could not conceive another child. In 1910 he made overtures to his wife to import two orphans from Britain but when his wife heard about the plan, she refused and said, "Your political friends will say that you bringing the orphans into Canada to be slaves."

"All right," Windsor said at the time. "It's that I'm away from home a lot and though the orphaned girls would be good company for you."

"So why don't you invite your nieces Erin and Margaret Carpenter, to come instead. Not only are they relatives, but teachers as well."

"And that is what Windsor did. He wrote Erin, Margaret and their parents, inviting the two teachers to come to Winnipeg and live with his family so that Wife Patricia would not be lonely.

At his home in Winnipeg, Windsor, Patricia, Erin and Margaret were discussing the war over dinner. Not only did they discuss James Buller's death, the sinking of the Lusitania, Petro joining the Royal Air Corps in London but also the Canadian Minister of Militia and National Defense in Borden's Conservative government, Colonel Sam Hughes.

'I think it's criminal that so many soldiers could be killed during the Battle of Ypres." Erin said.

Patricia agreed, "I think Colonel Hughes is stupid and insane."

"Why is that?" Margaret asked.

"The Colonel makes unilateral decisions without consulting the prime minister or cabinet members. That is one of the reasons."

"If Colonel Hughes is insane it is only moderately so." Margaret cut in.

"Why is that," Patricia said again.

"Because Hughes administering an $11-million budget and among other things. He is the one to approve the Ross rifle."

"That's a good point," Windsor said. "The rifle is good for single shots, but when fired in succession, the barrel heats up and sometimes explode. This is why 60,000 soldiers have died in Ypres. It's because of the Ross rifle."

And Windsor may have been right. The facts, rumors and condemnation of the Ross Rifle reverberated across Canada.

Then Erin asked Windsor, 'Why doesn't Canada use the flying machine like the one Petro is flying in England?"

"Because Colonel Hughes has no confidence in them. Although his department has purchased two from United States, they are still in crates kept in storage. You see, Colonel Hughes says aeroplanes or flying machines as you call them are the invention of the devil."

In the conversation that followed it was mentioned that Colonel Hughes was involved in a number of controversial issues. As an Orangeman, he imposed a highly unpopular ban on wet canteens in all militia corps and went out of his way to show disgust for anything Catholic or French.

There were charges both in the press and in the House of Commons that some of Hughes's appointees were growing rich through influence peddling and other forms of corruption. One of the allegations was that Windsor Co. Ltd. got a contract to supply Canadian troops with jam when in reality no fruit trees grew in Winnipeg.

Fortunately, Hughes's flamboyant but erratic star was rapidly fading. Prime Minister Borden appointed a Royal Commission to look into the irregularities in the purchase of arms and munitions and while subsequent finds were inconclusive,

Hughes continued to act independently after ignoring Borden's instructions and more than one, flagrantly defying the prime minister. Borden noted in his diary: "As if were a distinct and separate government itself. Hughes cannot remain in the government so I asked him to resign effective November 11, 1916," which he did. That was eight months after Winnipeg voted in favor of Prohibition. While the Windsor's, Erin and Margaret were discussing Sam Hughes, there was a knock on the front door and Windsor called out, "Come in."

It was Victoria Jackson and when she stepped inside said, "Good evening Mr. Windsor. I hope I didn't interrupt your dinner."

"You didn't. Please come inside," Windsor said motioning to the dining room.

I stopped to service your home with Mancan pyrohy, holubtsi and our complete line of soap products," Ms. Jackson proceeded.

As soon as Jackson mentioned the word Mancan Windsor burst out with anger. "No pyrohy, holubtsi or your darn soap."

"Why? They are the finest products made."

"You never told me that Mancan is operated by two Ukrainians."

"Calm down. We'll have the same as the last time," Patricia interrupted her husband, which was a repeat order.

"Why would you want to buy that stuff?" Windsor protested.

"I'll tell you why." Patricia answered.

"Okay, Why?"

"Why, because Mancan products are superior to the line of comparable products carried by the retail Windsor stores."

"But Windsor stores do not carry such delicious products"

"That's another reason we'll have a repeat order," Patricia said.

It was during December that Erin invited Margaret and Patricia to a Christmas concert at her school. While Margaret could not see she could hear the sounds of students performing in groups and individually. *The Nine Jolly Negroes* and *Two Little Maids* performed by the entire group pleased Margaret the most.

She also enjoyed *Jingle Bells* by the grade one class and *While Shepherds Watched Their Flocks* by those in grade eight.

There were several one act plays, recitations and children singing *Drink to Me with Thine Eyes*.

Penultametly, Santa Claus arrived with bags of candy and nuts that were distributed to the children. When Santa was through everyone sang *God Save the King*.

Once the concert was over Margaret said, "There was no reference made to Ukrainian Christmas traditions."

"You noticed that too." Erin replied "Why is that?"

"The school board wants it that way despite the fact Ukrainians are fighting for the retention of a bilingual school system."

"Why is that?" Margaret said again.

"I know why." Patricia joined in the conversation.

"So that Ukrainians assimilate more readily into the Canadian way of life."

"And do you want to know something else?" This time Patricia said, "What?"

Erin said, "The school board has instructed its teachers to use the strap on anyone who speaks Ukrainian in school.

CHAPTER THIRTEEN

Concentration Camp # 10 - January 1916

It got colder as the north wind swept across the Canadian prairie. Those in the Brandon Concentration Camp were issued army boots, flannel shirts, underwear and waterproof mackinaw. Those who worked in building railways or dirt roads were supplied with mitts also. The army garb served to drive home Pawlo state of captivity. Not only was he a prisoner, but also since Petro's escape a year ago, he had lost a good friend and a business partner.

At Christmas time, inmates received a book of coupons, each worth ten cents. These coupons were exchanged in the canteen for tobacco and oranges. Even so, Christmas in the Brandon Concentration Camp was the loneliest part in Pawlo's entire life. Erin did not visit because of the severe winter weather. The snow continued falling without let up. In several days it was knee-deep and every day it seemed to get deeper and deeper and the temperature dropped to as low as –40F. Notwithstanding the deep snow and the bitter cold the internees, guarded by soldiers armed with rifles, continued to work outside.

One redeeming feature about the winter was its short days. Before it got dark all the men quit work and returned to the barracks. After supper, they livened the barracks with chatter and amusements.

In all there were 1200 men in the camp. The majority were between twenty and thirty, the rest were from thirty to fifty. One third of them were Ukrainians from Galicia and there others were Croats, Poles, Germans and Hungarians. There were also about 100 Turks but they were lodged in a separate barrack.

In the evening, it was easy to tell who was of Ukrainian heritage because when their work was done they gathered for a singsong. There seemed to be no end to the number of songs they knew. Pawlo sang also so he could take his mind of his imprisonment, Mancan and Erin.

In other barracks prisoners made music on different instruments and danced the kolomyka and hopak. Mind you dancing with another man instead of a woman wasn't fashionable but it did take one's troublesome mind away from the burden of being a prisoner.

In another barrack several inmates were learning their parts for a theatrical performance of *Swatania Na Honorcharivsta*.

When the play was staged Pawlo went to see it but thought the actor who played the role of a young woman did not change his voice and neither the skirt he wore, and the wig of braided hair were of any help. In another barrack still, the Croats played their mandolins and sang the same melody over and over again, "Hai, hai, hai sikiru mi dai." Not everyone sang songs or played instruments. There was one inmate who sat in bunkhouse and read the Bible each evening while another with a pocketknife made a variety of carvings of high artistic quality. This particular Ukrainian inmate, not only did he make picture frames but also a violin from 365 pieces of wood glued together. To look at this prisoner one got the impression that he was a useless slouch, but he possessed remarkable talent for carving figurines also. His carved figure of Ketman Khmelyntsky mounted on horse with a mace in his hand reminded Pawlo of the statue of Khmelyntsky he once saw in Kiev.

"This prisoner is a true master of the art of carving," Pawlo thought and said to himself, "I wonder if I can buy the violin from him?" Pawlo played the violin when he lived in Lvov and admired Fritz Kreisler, the leading musician in Austria at the time.

"How much do you want for the violin?" Pawlo asked the inmate who identified himself as Mike Sokolosky. I would like to have it played when Erin Carpenter and I get married."

"It took six months to carve and glue the pieces together. Really, one can't put a value on it," Sokolosky replied and while handing the violin to Pawlo said, "Here, play it."

After playing several Ukrainian tunes Pawlo acknowledged, "It's no Stradivarius but close to it. How about if I pay you one hundred dollars as soon as we are out of jail, and in addition to the one hundred, I'll give you a job making pyrohy and holubtsi at the Mancan factory in Winnipeg."

"That sounds like a generous offer because jobs are difficult to find," Sokolosky said and continued, "On the other hand I do not know how to make pyrohy and holubtsi because my wife always makes them."

"Don't worry about that. At one time you didn't know how to make violins either. As a matter of fact, I'll also hire your wife and you will have double income."

"To me you appear to be an honest man. It's a deal, but on one condition," Sokolosky said.

"What's the condition?"

"That I play the violin at your wedding."

The two inmates shook hands.

Brandon Concentration Camp # 10
Easter weekend 1916

When the 1916 /1917 winter came to an end
and Easter arrived, Pawlo and the other
Ukrainian inmates were disheartened because
there was no priest to celebrate a church
service in the concentration camp. Only now
and then someone would softly say,
"Khrystos Vokres."
Each inmate was weighed down in his own
misery. For Pawlo Easter was an important
religious festival. He recalled how he use to
enjoy making multi-colored Easter eggs with
his mother in the Old Country.
This was done during the forty days of Lent
before Easter. Pawlo recalled going to a
church service and the priest at the time
saying, "Christ has risen. He is truly risen."
Pawlo also recalled how Easter breakfast
began with eating of an egg that his mother
pealed and his father cut into piece and
passing them to members of the family and
saying, "This is the symbol of life at Easter.
Eat and rejoice."

At this particular moment Pawlo could not rejoice because he was watching a train arrive with new internees. As soon as the internees got off the train they were taken to empty barracks.

Pawlo was appalled by their appearance, as their faces were drawn and yellow in color. They all looked hungry, exhausted, haggard, cold, young and ill-humoured, without exception.

"This is a frightful sight for an Easter Sunday. No human should look like that," Pawlo said to another inmate and then while the new internees were rounded up, he spoke to several. Their speech was difficult to understand for the spoke with difficulty, some through tears. All those Pawlo talked with complained that they had not had any food that day. Hearing this, Pawlo got busy and collected several coupons to buy food for them from the canteen. Each inmate donated as many coupons as he could and Pawlo exchanged them for oranges and chocolates, which he gave, each arrival.

For supper the new arrivals were served the same food as Pawlo and the other internees, but some had lost their appetite and could not eat.

After Pawlo had listened to their complaints, he found that the new arrivals were transferred from another concentration camp where they were forced to do hard labor. Pawlo was also told that at the Spirit Lake camp in northern Quebec, two men were shot while trying to escape and twenty others died from tuberculosis and pneumonia.

On Easter Monday, the new arrivals asked for a day off because it was a holy day for them. The Major, however, when he heard the request responded with, "The hell with your holy day. Last year inmates worked on the Feast of Annunciation."

Immediately after breakfast the new internees were asked to join the other inmates to go to work, but they refused and stayed in their barracks. By 9:00 a. m. officials summoned the new internees one by one to the office, and demanded an explanation why they were refusing to work. When it was an individual's turn he was asked, "Why didn't you go to work?"

One individual, more haggard than the rest, replied, "You did not capture me on a battlefield. I came to Canada not to fight a war but to earn a living and enrich this country with my labors."

When drilled further, the internee replied, "I always observe Easter Monday as a holy day just like my ancestors did. They shed their blood for the privilege of observing this day. But you do not let us observe this holiday and you mock us besides. You have desecrated the holy day and for that you will have to answer to God."

Other internees had similar objections and some even held back on the Third Commandment for defense and declared that God's commandments took precedence over orders from the Concentration Camp administration and no one is a slave forced to work on a holy day. All the men vowed they would rather suffer more harm than work on an Easter Monday.

In the end an internee stood up and declared in the name of the entire group, "Major, because you are forcing us to work on a holy day we are not going to ever work in this concentration camp."

Major Matheson gave the new internees a short talk and told them that the men in barracks before them had worked faithfully over the past two years and obediently discharged their duties.

"They received good meals, clothing and twenty-five cents a day and were satisfied. Will you work or not?"

From all around came the resounding answer, "We will not work!"

Major Matheson then came out of his office, and while he was away. Pawlo expressed concern to the arrivals that they were laying themselves open for further hardship by refusing to work.

The haggard new internee replied, "We are not afraid of persecution," and recounted instances, which his group experienced every time they refused to work in the camp they were interned before.

"Our food rations were immediately reduced by one-half, the straw from the bunks was removed and the warm clothing was taken away.

"We were forced to run, fall to the ground and rise to our feet again repeatedly while being flogged. We were forced to carry fifty-pound bags of sand a distance of thirty miles. Our daily food ration continued to be progressively reduced until we had only bread and water.

One hundred of our men were transferred to the Brandon Concentration Camp and what is going to happen to those we is left behind, we do not know. But we know this; we are not going to work on an Easter Monday."

Pawlo admired the decision the internees' had made and their determination to stand up for their rights. "Your spirit is praiseworthy and you put us, long time internees, to shame for our submissiveness and slavish acquiescence to servility. We feel the same way as you do but with the exception of Petro Czorny, who was successful in escaping, we remained silent."

By noon, all the men who arrived on the train that night were summoned one by one to the Major's office again, but they still refused to work. Of the one hundred, only ten pleaded illness and were allowed to return to the barracks. The rest were punched, pushed and shoved forcibly out of the barracks by soldiers who later assembled the internees into a group. Other soldiers arrived and surrounded the captives on all sides.

Major Matheson and Lieutenant Coleman emerged from the office and ordered the internees to proceed marching.

The unique parade moved slowly passed the warehouses and forward toward the direction where Pawlo and 500 other long-time internees watched what was happening.
As the parade approached them Pawlo called out to the internees next to him, "Hey, fellow prisoners, these men are marching to their torture. They are bothers, let's help them!"

At first only Pawlo made the move, but then suddenly, rest of the inmates in the group followed and blocked the advance of the procession. Pawlo walked up to Major Matheson while a guard standing next to him pulled out a gun and fired it into the air.
And then, used the same gun to strike Pawlo over the head knocking him to the ground.
And said, "Take this you son of a bitch,"
The internees, long-time and new arrivals alike, became furious with what the guard did and raised uproar by shouting insults at him.
"Kill the guard, kill the Major" one internee shouted.
"Beat him up! Stone him!" shouted another.
"Shame! Shame!" other internees agreed.
What loneliness Major Matheson must have felt as there was confusion among the guards.
The Major gave a signal to sound the trumpet, but instead, Pawlo recovered and urged the

prisoners to return to their barracks and the soldiers back to the office.

The incident wasn't without its toll, however, as several internees were injured before they managed to reach the barracks by pursuing troops who had left their mark on each of the internees. A bayonet had grazed Pawlo's arm and for several days he felt the pain although the wound wasn't serious.

Cork, Ireland - Easter Monday 1916

On the same Easter Monday, 1916, there was an uprising of a different kind in Ireland. Erin and Margaret were frequently on the phone with their parents in Cork and what they were told wasn't surprising. The Citizens' Army, the Volunteers, and the Brotherhood were now united and became the Irish Republican Army. Civil war seemed imminent. Republicans and Socialists became weary of the starvation wages and poor working conditions.

On Easter Monday they came out in open insurrection, seized the centre of Dublin and proclaimed an Irish Republic. Numbering only one hundred men, they were defeated in a week of bitter fighting in which a great part of the centre of the city was destroyed by fire and artillery.

At first the public reaction was one of shocked hostility, but a long-drawn out series of executions of leaders, culminating in the shooting of the crippled Sean McDermott and Socialist leader James Connelly, brought reaction of sympathy and support.

Connolly was dying of gangrene from a leg shattered in the fighting and had to be propped up in a chair before a firing squad.

In a subsequent conversation with her mother in Ireland Erin asked, "And how is Thomas McCurtain doing?"

"Well, he won't be dancing at your wedding."

"Why, Mom?"

"Because he was murdered in his home, before the eyes of his wife and children."

"By whom?"

"By a pair of blackened gunmen," her mother replied and went on to say that the clandestine IRA now had 50,000 members.

"How about the British army?"

"The British army no longer is able to find Irishmen to fight the IRA and have recruited a special task force in England."

What Anne Carpenter had said was correct.
This much feared and hated little army, the
Black and Tans; found itself half besieging
and half besieged by a desperate hateful
enemy it seldom saw. It was a war of
darkened colors, silent streets; dark shapes in
trench coats hurrying through the fog, the
sudden terrifying sound of marchers in the
night. No man could ever be sure his next
wary step around a quiet street corner would
not be his last.

Brandon Concentration Camp # 10
Easter Monday 1916

A short time after the internees in the Brandon
Concentration Camp refused to work a
Special Commission, made up of Judge John
Hall and two lawyers arrived in the city to
investigate the Uprising.
At the hearing Ukrainian internees stressed
their point of view that they were not
prisoners of war and therefore should not
submit to forced labor. They also felt they
should not work on a holy day such as an
Easter Monday.
Judge Hall was an amiable white-haired man
who ran his hearing with informality.

He was a man who knew Canadian history and although he seemed to take his assignment casually, kept a firm grip on the proceedings. His two associates, in their fifties, neatly dressed in dark suites, spoke little.

There were many witnesses called and when it was Pawlo's turn he asked the Judge, "What crimes have I committed against Canada? Take me for instance; I'm twenty six years old and in a Gulag. I can't join the Canadian army even if I wanted too."

Near the end of his exchange of words with Pawlo the Judge said, "Mr. Bilyi, in your own words tell the Commission what happened on the day the internees clashed with the soldiers."

"Your honor," Pawlo began and went on, "It was on Easter Monday morning and the Major refused the new internees a day off. I saw inmates punched, pushed and shoved by soldiers with bayonets after the prisoners refused to work. Later more soldiers arrived and grouped the men into files of four and ordered them to march…"

"Please continue," the Judge said as Pawlo paused to recall the sequence of events that led to the clash with the soldiers.

"Later Major Matheson and Lieutenants Coleman and emerged and were leading the internees who arrived Easter Sunday to torture."

"How do you know the men were going to be tortured?"

"Because I have been in similar marches before and when I asked the Major not to torture these men because they were weak, some sick, the Major pulled out a gun and fired into the air. Using the same gun he then struck me across my head and I collapsed to the ground."

"And then what happened?"

"The internees were disgusted with what the Major had done and were going to attack him and the soldiers. I intervened so they shouted obscenities at the Major instead."

"And."

"And when the internees were returning to their barracks soldiers followed and used their bayonets."

The Judge looked up as if he expected a rebuttal from the Major or questions from the other Commission members but there were none.

So he continued, "Were any of the internees injured?"

"There were. And several were hospitalized."

"How many?"

"Ten."

"Those sent to the hospital were they in serious condition?'

"Not serious but I know several suffered injuries to their necks, and arms and one is in danger of losing an eye."

Pawlo blinked and ran a hand through his hair. "It was the right eye."

"And how do you know it was the right eye?"

"I'm certain it was the right because of friend of mine, Margaret Carpenter, first lost the sight in her right eye before she became totally blind. It was something I could relate too."

All Ukrainian internees had an opportunity to say what they wanted to say and when they were finished, the Judge spoke for thirty minutes. Pawlo stiffened as he was sitting with the internees and thought it was certain he was going to spend time in solitary confinement, but it wasn't the case after the Judge Hall said, "It comes as a great surprise to some Galician's that they are enemies of the British Empire and remained shocked at being prisoners of war.

Knowing the background and history of Ukrainian people I agree that most of them are not dangerous saboteurs."

Then looking at the prisoners from one to the other, the Judge went on, "Most of you have spent up to two years of your life in this concentration camp because someone didn't like you and the discrimination and prejudiced Canadian government policy.

What has happened here is a national disgrace and I agree with Major General Otter when he recently said, quote, 'With so many abled men imprisoned and posing no threat to security, I recommend that the thousands of harmless Austrians be released into the work force,' end of quote.

I agree with Major General Otter who has recommend that most of the internees in the Brandon Concentration Camp be released from incarceration immediately."

Brandon Concentration Camp # 10
August 31, 1916

By August 31, 1916 all Majors and Lieutenants, with the exception of Lieutenant Crosthwait, were discharged.

News of the Judge's decision spread across Canada and United States and then to all parts of the world with editorials.

Ukrainians in Winnipeg could find coverage in the *Ukrainian Voice* and *Svaboda* which was published in New Jersey.

Winnipeg – September 1, 1916

The announcement also made English headlines in the Masses in New York and the *Tribune* and *Free Press* in Winnipeg.
"We should never take freedom for granted," Pawlo said to Dr. Kozak after Pawlo was released, after spending nearly two years at the Brandon Concentration Camp, and returned to Winnipeg. Following his visit with Dr. Kozak and a tour of the Mancan operation, Pawlo met with the employees and thanked them for working under difficult circumstances. Next he met with Erin in the Windsor home.
As soon as Pawlo and d Erin finished embracing, Erin said pointing to a child on the floor, "This is our baby. Little Patricia will be two in July. Isn't she pretty?"
Pawlo slowly inspected the child and said, "She has your mouth and nose."
"Little Patricia looks like both of us," Erin replied, picked up the child and gave it to Pawlo to hold.

Pawlo admired the child and noticed that the diaper had come off and her bottom was bare. "She'll catch cold," he said.

Erin adjusted the diaper and turned towards the kitchen. "It's time to feed her."

Pawlo watched as Erin mixed a dish of baby food and warmed up a bottle of milk. "I breast fed her for a month and when I returned to school I changed to formula."

After the child was fed and placed in a jolly jumper Erin said, "I do like the name Patricia."

"Congratulations, so do I. It must make your aunt happy."

Minutes later Erin began to weep.

"Don't cry honey. Everything will turn out all right. Have you given up teaching?"

"I haven't and I must admit Aunt Patricia doesn't mind babysitting. Surprisingly Uncle Henry doesn't mind the child either. That's when he's at home and not in Ottawa."

Pawlo and Erin kept talking for another one-half hour when Erin said, "Pawlo do you really love me?"

"It has been my dream for you to be my wife ever since we met on the S. S. Christiana as it sailed from Liverpool. The question now is when should our marriage take place?"

Erin didn't expect Pawlo to be so forthright.
"If it's going to be a double-ring ceremony
with Petro and Margaret too, I suggest we
hold off until the war is over and Petro is back
from the war."

"The way the war is going it could be a long,
long time."

"Could be, but it is you that said good things
are worth waiting for."

At that precise moment Margaret walked into
the room and said, "I thought I heard a
familiar voice. Is that you Pawlo?"

"It's me, Pawlo," Pawlo said and sat next to
Margaret on a couch. "It's nice to see you."

"And it's nice to hear you," she replied.

"Have you heard from Petro?"

"I have. Now that he's with the Royal Flying
Corps he writes frequently."

Margaret updated Pawlo on Petro and how he
escaped the Brandon Concentration Camp,
survived the sinking of the Lusitania and him
joining the Corps.

"Now can you update me on what's
happening to the war since I was interned?"
"Pawlo asked.

"I can't but Erin can."

Erin proceeded, "I'll summarize the war as quickly as I can. A revolution broke out in Russia…"

As soon as Erin finished talking about what had happened in Russia to this point, Pawlo asked, "And how are the Germans reacting to the revolution?"

"The Germans from what I gather are extremely delighted by the internal disorders and are encouraging groups of extremists, the Bolsheviks, under the leadership of Vladmir Lenin (1870-1924) to return to Russia from exile in Switzerland."

Later, commenting on the chain of events that led to the revolution, Erin said the Western Allies are worried about the influence of the revolution on Russia's continuation of the war and sent a special mission to Russia. These missions included prominent socialists who are expected to establish friendly relations with the new Russian government."

"And how is Canada doing?"

"Oh, even I know that," Margaret cut in, "Canada is having a difficult time."

"Why is that?"

"Because Uncle Harry says few men are enlisting into the army and Prime Minister Borden is thinking of bringing conscription."

Shortly after Pawlo's release, editors of six Ukrainian newspapers wrote An Address to the People of Canada that was published in English newspapers and attempted to correct the misapprehension of Anglo Canadians about Ukrainian political sentiments.

When Windsor read the article, he burst out with laughter. "Ukrainians are always crying because they were persecuted by the Polacks in Galicia, in Russia by the Russians and in Canada by English fanatics. Ukrainians are nothing but a bunch of liars. It is regrettable Clifford Sifton and Prime Minister Laurier encouraged them to come to Canada." When Windsor said those words it was the same day that Mancan was holding a rally in Winnipeg. Distributors from Victoria to Halifax were there to hear Dr. Kozak pay tribute to Pawlo and Petro. Each time their names were mentioned there was a burst of applause.

Dr. Kozak said he was delighted to have looked after the affairs of Mancan during Petro and Pawlo's absence and grateful many distributors were involved in marketing its products.

The theme of the rally was Why I Should Be in Mancan and featured some of the leading distributors as guest speakers. When called upon the stage a distributor from British Columbia gave testament the products he was marketing by saying, "All I have to do is remind you of the present world situation and that some people generally do not have security. But even if things are booming people still get fired, let go for any reason." Next a distributor from New Brunswick said, "And you know people have accidents that cause them to lose income. I don't have to remind you that death takes the wage earner away many times leaving the wife and family to ship for themselves. With Mancan you call the shots. You are rewarded by the efforts you put into your business."

A distributor from Ontario spoke next, "Everyone needs up line support so I find sponsors.

The biggest reason people may be reluctant to work for Mancan is fear of failing. Not me. I feel failing is the number one reason why people can't succeed. I ask you to forget about being afraid to make mistakes. Sooner or later you will hit a home run."

A distributor from Manitoba took the podium next and excitedly said, "All I can tell you is that my Mancan business is growing. Sure, sometimes I get frustrated but it's worth it. When I was in the 15% level I often wondered where all my time was spent and where the money was. I'm telling you something. When the money does start coming it doesn't trickle in. It's building up behind a dam and it builds and builds until all of a sudden the dam bursts and the money starts rolling in."

When it was Victoria Jackson's turn to speak she walked up to the podium and said among other things, "About the Mancan System. Each morning I write out my goals and dreams. I inspire myself and then I inspire others. I have no time for philosophizing or negatives. It's important to know where I'm going so I write out my goals before I go to bed.

If I can sell pyrohy and holubtsi to an Anglo-Saxon Conservative member of parliament I'm certain you can sell them to almost anyone."

There were other distributors who spoke too, many of whom were presented plaques for achievement, holiday trips to the tropics and others encouraged to hang in and put in extra effort. In the end the rally was one of the best Mancan ever had.

Before the distributors went their separate ways Pawlo encouraged them by saying, "Go forth and sell Canada the Mancan way. Don't worry if you get a hit or a strike. The important thing is that you swing the bat."

Vimy Ridge, France – April 1917

In 1917 the war entered a new phase in which the whole world was involved in one-way or another. It was the year United States entered the war and Russia dropped out. It was the same year Canadian troops captured Vimy Ridge in France on Easter Monday, the 9th of April, 1917 but not before 10,000 soldiers lost their lives and John Windsor became a hero. Because of poor communication and rigid censorship few Canadians thought of the war in the same terms as the young Windsor. He characterized it best when he wrote home after Pawlo was released from the Brandon Detention Camp, and described the war in terms of blood, mud, lice, diarrhea, smell of excrement and decaying corpses in the trenches.

That night of April 8 was Easter Sunday and for once John could write home an encouraging letter. The strength of the Canadian Corps, including all attached British troops stood at 170,000. Fifteen of its assault moved into positions through tunnels from Arras. By 4:00 a. m. Easter Monday every battalion was in place, most of them no more than 100 yards from the enemy. It rained on them most of the night and then in the cold of the early morning rain changed to sleet and snow.

In the last minute of the cold night before the attack, the artillery finished its work. Besides the usual curtain of high explosives on the forward position, a heavy barrage of gas shells was thrown into the German rear.
The greatest and most decisive casualties of the gas were not men but horses.
They died in hundreds and when the infantry attack began the German communications systems were in chaos.
The troops at the front ran short of ammunition. The artillery had no means of locomotion. The main allied rush across the sleet-drenched hillside therefore was given a chance to succeed.

On some parts of the ridge the very high depth and safety of the German trenches now betrayed their defenders. With the Allied artillery fire stopped it took a long time to pour into the tiny strip of No Man's Land. In the first rush nearly 3500 Germans surrendered. In one of the many impregnable tunnels 150 German soldiers came up dazed and half-dressed their hands aloft.

The four Canadian divisions in the attack proceeded up the slope, some throwing grenades, some carrying guns, majority armed with bayonets and rifles shooting through the rising fog and snow against the enemy they could not see Not surprisingly the Canadians achieved facets of great courage and John Windsor was one of the soldiers.
The young Windsor, an officer, with only two men to support, leaped into one of the enemy trenches and captured two officers and fifteen other men with different ranks. By Easter Monday the snow had stopped and those who had to burst through No Man's Land of Vimy and gained its height could look out on the great plain beyond.
In a letter home John Windsor described the sight this way: "When the snow stopped falling I saw a remarkable sight.

The air was suddenly clean and clear filled with spring sunshine.

The high ground was covered with English-speaking troops standing about in four large groups. For a moment the artillery fire cased on both sides and complete silence fell on the battlefield, as if it was lost in wonder. The battle itself seemed to hold its breath."

Though Vimy Ridge was considered as one of the great military successes of the war it was not a decisive victory because the Allies were simply running out of soldiers.

The capture of Vimy Ridge, when it was finally over, cost the Allies 150,000 men. Many of the French soldiers would not fight any longer and the fifty divisions either mutinied out right or threatened to mutiny. There were soldiers who preferred possible death by court martial to certain death by the German gun.

Margaret was correct when she said earlier, "I think conscription is about to take place." Prime Minister Borden too knew the enlistment rate could have to be stepped up if Canadian force was to be maintained in Europe.

Although he still had not claimed Canadian citizenship Peter Black was making flights over Germany with the Royal Air Corps. The plane he used at the time was even more primitive than the tank used by the Allies below. Initially the slow aircraft was used only for most rudimentary kind of reconnaissance and Peter Black found himself in the same piece of the sky as German pilots who drew their revolver and duel it out as in movies Hollywood started to make.

Later, Peter Black was armed with a carbine and then with a machine gun, and finally the plane itself became a flying gun with cartridge belts with it.

CHAPTER FOURTEEN

Ottawa – April, 1917

"Canada is running short of manpower!"
Prime Minister Borden told parliament,
concerned about the Canadian war efforts.
"Battle losses have been grievous and
recruiting has dropped steady for a year now.
Even using the Fifth Division for
reinforcements, it is becoming increasingly
difficult to keep four divisions already
committed to strength."

In the spring of 1917 Prime Minister Borden
returned from the Imperial Conference in
London convinced that compulsory military
service, something he had consistently
rejected until then, could no longer be
avoided. The announcement touched of an
emotional outcry that shook the country from
coast to coast to coast.. Many individuals,
most farm and labor organizations were
staunchly against conscription but most of the
opposition came from the province of
Quebec. The legacy of Sam Hughes had an
important influence on this. The former
Minister of Militia had gone out of his way to
taunt and anger the Roman Catholic Church
in Quebec.

In spite of the noble combat record of the Vandoos no attempt had been made to place volunteers in French-speaking units. Colonel Sam Hughes seemed to think it was good for them to learn to speak English.

And many of the recruiting agents in Quebec were Protestant ministers. Still more provocative was the legislation enacted in Ontario and Manitoba to restrict or eliminate the teaching of French language in provincial schools.

"Why should we die for an empire and a country that denies us justice and the constitutional right?" many French Canadians asked the prime minister.

A legion of Quebecois spoke out against the conscription from pulpits, platforms and rostrums but two were more prominent than the rest: they belonged to familiar but very defiant antagonists of Borden – Wilfred Laurier and Henry Bourassa. Laurier, constantly moderate, temperate and cooperative toward the war, from the beginning had supported the Conservative government and even agreed to extend the life of parliament by a year in the conviction that circumstances required a temporary end to partisan politics.

Laurier urged the youth of his native province to enlist. Seeing that conscription would put a man overseas against his will, Laurier did not view compulsory service as a practical solution.

"How many men will conscription bring in?" he asked Borden and when Borden was groping for words he answered his own question, "Just a few slackers, exactly the same as in England."

Bourassa was less restrained, far more intemperate. If he did not actually urge rebellion in the editorial of the Le Devoir, he acknowledged it to be an almost inevitable result.

And his chief lieutenant, Armand Lavergne, advocated disobedience to the Compulsory Service Bill.

"Vive la liberte!" Lavergne shouted to a large audience in Montreal. "Vive l'independence!" Outside Quebec Laurier's support fell day by day. Clifford Sifton defected again to Borden. So did many supporters of Laurier's in Ontario and the Maritimes. Borden decided to consolidate his position by creating a Union Government in which ten pro-conscription Liberals accepted posts as cabinet ministers and parliamentary assistants.

Still the Prime Minister felt to "Go to the Country" on the issue of conscription.

The resulting election campaign in 1917 was a bitter one, steeped with emotions and passion. Borden used every means open to him to ensure the results he wanted. Mothers, wives, and sisters of men in the armed forces, who could be expected to endorse conscription, were given the right to vote by Act of Parliament. Immigrants from Germany and the Austro-Hungarian Empire, who had been in Canada for less than fifteen years and might oppose conscription, were summarily disenfranchised.

While the election campaign was taking place there were fears among the Anglo Saxons in Winnipeg that his involvement with the Mancan Corporation, because of his Ukrainian heritage, many thought that Pawlo was connected with the Russian Revolution. Involved or not Ukrainian newspapers were censored and those published in Canada had to be printed in Ukrainian and English columns.

"It's just like in the Austro-Hungarian Empire," Pawlo said to Jimmy McKernan who came to visit him in the Mancan manufacturing plant and headquarters.

"Now you know what it's like to be imprisoned," McKernan said.

"Imprisoned but determined."

"Determined to do what?"

"To make Mancan the largest sales company and find justice for Ukrainians living in Canada." Pawlo answered and then asked a question of his own, "Jimmy, how do you enjoy working for the city of Winnipeg?"

"Every time our union asks Mayor Gray and City Council for an increase in pay the Mayor says we are agitators. That is why I have joined the Socialist Democratic Party."

Pawlo may not have had the highest I Q in Winnipeg but he realized that if he joined a political party he would be walking a thin line with many of his customers and distributors. "I'd rather be a student of human behavior." he said and asked McKernan if he was a Communist."

"Not a Communist but a Socialist," he candidly replied.

The first thing Pawlo did since his release from the Brandon Concentration Camp and as the chief executive officer of Mancan, was to accelerate the mass marketing of pyrohy, holubtsi and soap across Canada at a time when everyone seemed to be talking about doom and gloom, low wages, high freight rates, a revolution in Russia and conscription in Canada. He called for a mass rally of distributors to be held in Winnipeg on the same day that the federal election was to be held. The French Canadians in particular didn't place many orders, as they were upset with the conscription issue. They were too concerned about their own rights to be over worried about what was happening to Mancan or minorities. Quebec nationals soon began to berate Prime Minister Borden. For example Cardinal Begin said, "This military service is not only a blow to the rights of the church of Christ. Independently of its domain but it constitutes a fatal obstacle to the recruiting ministers of God, shepherds of souls, as well as that of the staff of clerical teachers, and through this fact, creates in our society, an event much more worse which it is alleged to attempt to remedy."

Similarly the influential Archbishop Bruchesi supported registration but denounced conscription when he said, "We are nearing a racial crises of war."
Canada had not been so been divided since Wolfe and Moncalm fought on the Plains of Abraham. Some Quebec newspapers urged Quebec to withdraw from Confederation and newspapers that were published in English were threatened to be destroyed by fire.

On Election Day the Board of Trade Auditorium in Winnipeg was filled to capacity with Mancan distributors despite the fact there so many people against conscription. Many had voted in advance polls. There was a super-charged atmosphere surrounded by music, cheers, glitter and excitement as the distributors gathered to acquire information and skills they needed to build stronger and more profitable businesses. There were speeches, testimonials, seminars and presentations geared to deliver practical information that would make Mancan distributors respected members of their communities.

When Pawlo spoke at the rally banquet he
received a tumultuous applause. He told
those gathered that Mancan had gone through
difficult times due to his and Petro's
interment.

"Despite the hardship the little pyrohy,
holubtsi and soap company in Winnipeg just
kept growing. As Canada has learned about
the Mencan phenomenon so have we.
Perhaps because we have been forced to
defend and justify our goal Mancan has
carried out business deep into the unexplored
country. We have watched as ordinary people,
no matter what their ethnic origin; continue to
embrace the Mancan opportunity. We have
learned with proper support the Mancan
Corporation and its hundreds of distributors
have recourses, the will, and the spirit to carry
our hope to every heart that permits a choice.
We are going where no one has been and we
accept the risk of being first and best."
Here the distributors let out another burst of
applause more deafening than the first.
Pawlo continued. "That is why I'm delighted
tonight to announce several important
changes that will improve our direction in
which we are going.

First, Dr. Kozak has been appointed vice-president of Mancan until further notice. Also appointed to vice-presidency ranks are Erin and Margaret Carpenter and Nathan Tarnoff from Chicago who will be in charge of United States sales and Ms. Jackson, regional manager for the province of Manitoba."

There was applause and when it died down Pawlo continued, "I have another major announcement to make. On January 1, 1917 Mancan, besides marketing pyrohy, holubtsi and soap products, will venture into catalogue shopping with over 200 articles, ranging from overalls to light bulbs, from lipstick to furniture. Eaton's is doing it and we will do it better."

Here the distributors gave Pawlo a standing ovation. They knew people enjoyed shopping through a catalogue. As soon as the ovation died down a messenger appeared on the stage and handed Pawlo a piece of paper.

"There's other news most of you have been waiting to hear," Pawlo said and edged in closer to the microphone. He wanted to be certain what was written on the paper was correct so he read the note first to himself and then to his audience.

"Election polls have closed several hours ago and the Union Government of Prime Minister Borden has swept eight of the nine provinces in a great show of strength. Only Quebec voted against conscription."

His personal re-election and conscription approval made Windsor a happy man. He celebrated the occasion with a party of loyal supporters at his residence.

There were no horses tied to a fence or bicycles leaning against his home. Most everyone who came drove a Model T Ford, an Oldsmobile or a Buick.

Among those present in the victory celebration were politicians, bankers and executives of railway companies. There were also representatives from grain, wholesale and mercantile firms. The Mayor was there and it seemed that anyone who was a 'Who' and Anglo Saxon in Winnipeg, was there.

The guests began arriving shortly after the election results were known and welcomed at the front door by Windsor personally and his wife Patricia. Once the re-acquaintances and self-plaudits were made, Erin escorted the guests downstairs where in one corner stood a table with food and drinks.

A three-piece band was on hand to provide entertainment by playing popular tunes of the day.

As soon as a good number of guests had gathered and were chatting among themselves, Windsor exclaimed to a waiter, "You may now bring out the champagne."

As everyone, dressed in their Sunday best, drank and chewed niblets of food, a railway executive was talking with a banker and said, "The railways are having poor year. I believe railways should be subsidized by the government."

"Is that so?" the banker replied. "Ever since the war started banks haven't had it so good."

In another corner a metal fabricating executive complained to the Mayor that the Trades and Labor Congress wanted to negotiate a master contract on behalf of all the craft unions and he did not approve.

"The middle class will be destroyed if that happens," the metal fabricating executive said and Mayor Gray agreed by answering, "And so will the Anglo Saxons."

The Mayor lifted a drink to his lips and continued, "City Hall employees too are negotiating for higher wages.

I understand some have expressed interest in the One Big Union."

A shopkeeper then walked up to Windsor and said, "Soldiers returning from the battlefields are demanding jobs presently held by the aliens."

"I have that problem in my stores too," Windsor replied. "I can understand the situation however, and that is why I have fired several of my German and Ukrainian employees and hired soldiers. After all they fought for this country."

A woman in a low cut dress, walked by which caught Windsor's attention and said, "How charming you look tonight. Thank you for Voting gor me and conscription."

"It was a pleasure," the woman said. "To be candid with you it was a decision I mauled over for a week."

A short time later, Margaret was brought down a flight of stairs and her aunt, Patricia, introduced her to the guests.

"Now that the band is having a break, let's have another drink and listen to my niece, Margaret Carpenter, play the piano," Windsor said, "Hey waiter!"

At first Margaret was reluctant to go in front of an audience but after coaxing sat at a piano and played *Twelfth Street Rag*, a popular hit that year.

When she finished playing everyone clapped with enthusiasm. Many of the guests did not realize that Margaret, although blind, could play the piano so well.

"What else does she do?" the Mayor asked and Patricia Windsor replied, "Margaret also writes short stories about Ukrainian women and is working on a Broadway-like drama."

"Ukrainian women? That should be funny." the Mayor said and then mimicked one. After he was through mimicking the Mayor asked Margaret, "Can you play another tune?"

She did and after several more drinks some of the younger guests gathered around Margaret and one asked, "Can you accompany us in a sing-along?"

"I'll try my best," Margaret replied and ten men and women sang *Darktown Strutters Ball*, Liza Jane and *For Me and My Gal*.

Soon most of the guests and older alike *joined* in and sang other songs: *It's A Long Way To Tipperary*, *Keep The Home Fires Burning* and ended the party with a rousing Hail, Hail, The Gang Is All Here.

When it was past 3:00 a. m. the guests went home.

After its preliminaries, conscription turned out to be just as noisy as the Windsor celebration. There were categories of exemption and when the Act went into force the hearing of appeals took more time than swearing in and training new soldiers. It was not only the French Canadians who tried to evade the draft but also farmers' sons had been granted exemption under certain conditions and when they were refused the farmers stirred up demonstrations.

In Winnipeg, a group of farmers paraded through the streets shouting anti-conscription slogans and waving placards with the words: Conscription Is A Conspiracy Of the Rich And Powerful Against the Lowly, Every Man Taken Away From The Farmer Destroys The Power Of Canada To Feed The Men In The Front, Every Man Taken From A Canadian Farm Makes More Terrible The Cry Of Starving Children For Whom Men Are Fighting For and Do You Wish To Enslave Canada's Mankind To Help The Aristocrats?

Soon, there was much hostility to the French-speaking as there was to those who came to Canada from the Austria-Hungarian Empire. In Quebec there were disturbances as angry young anti-constructionists assaulted soldiers from Ontario with axe handles and hunting knives. The climax arrived when four civilians were killed and half a dozen soldiers wounded. Order was eventually restored but the young Quebecois fled by the hundreds into the Lurentian hills. Some were heavily armed and dared police and soldiers to come and get them.

Pawlo resolved to devote all his energy to the Mancan Corporation and to earning a better standard of living for himself and his distributors. He consulted with Erin and on one occasion she said to him, "To start, let's decorate your apartment where Little Patricia and I can live in."

"An excellent idea."

The apartments run down condition disappointed Erin. There was blistered paint, broken glass and dust everywhere and she noticed that the plaster on the ceilings had major cracks.

"We'll have to fill in all the cracks and paint and wallpaper the entire apartment. It's a mess. It's a pigsty." Erin said.

Then she noticed the floors needed scrubbing. "You can do that while go and purchase the wallpaper and the paint," Erin continued.

As soon as Erin returned and they had started stripping the wall in the bedrooms, they looked out the second story window and saw a soldier arguing with an elderly man.

"Look!" Pawlo exclaimed, "That's Dr. Kozak's father. He's being abused by a soldier."

Pawlo immediately took a flight of stairs that led to the outside, and when he reached the spot where the soldier was arguing with the Senior Kozak, he said to the soldier, "Why are you abusing this man who hardly speaks English?"

"Because he's a Hunky." the soldier replied.

"Listen." Pawlo said. "He's over seventy years of age. Is there another reason?"

"Yes, because like many other soldiers I'm unemployed."

Pawlo's and the soldier's eyes met.

"If I knew you weren't drunk I'd say you are a bum. Run along."

"I know my uniform may not be pressed and I may be a bit intoxicated but remember this," the solder said.

"Remember what?

"You didn't fight at Ypres or Vimy Ridge. You must be the man across the street that runs Mancan?"

"I am. My name is Pawlo Bilyi. What's yours?"

"I'm Private Victor Jackson. With a name like Bilyi you must be a Communist?"

"Look," Pawlo said for the second time.

"You better leave before I call the police."

After further arguing the soldier said, "Police? Police in Winnipeg are working for a starving wage, that's why they are going on strike soon."

After several more ping-pong like exchanges the soldier finally said, "Okay I'll go but the Veterans Association is going to hear about this."

"That you have abused an elderly man?"

"No,"

"What then?"

"That a soldier can't find work."

"And what else?"

"Ukrainian employers won't fire aliens so we can take their place."

"Instead of harassing employers why don't you become a Mancan distributor?"

"Mancan? Distributor?" Victor Jackson said.

"That's what my sister Victoria is doing and she's very good at it."

As soon as Victor Jackson expressed interest in being a Mancan distributor and was handed a sales kit he became animated and said, "I'll be a diamond category within a month and sponsor unemployed soldiers."

The following week when Erin finished decorating the apartment she said to Pawlo, "Now, isn't this better? Little Patricia and I will move over the weekend."

"That will be great," Pawlo said. "As far as decorating the apartment is concerned you were great too. You shouldn't be a teacher but an interior decorator."

Erin laughed at the compliment but she didn't laugh for long because Pawlo hung up a painting by an unknown artist on the living room wall and she said, "There's something about that picture that isn't right."

The painting showed a Ukrainian woman teaching a child to read by candlelight.

"What is the matter?" Pawlo asked.

"The painting doesn't make sense."

"How did you reach that conclusion?"

"Because in my experience as a teacher, it's the father who teaches a child to read."

"Always."

"Yes, always."

"How can you tell?"

"Because all Ukrainian women I have met, not one can read."

"Not only should you be an interior decorator but a critic for the newspaper as well," Pawlo said. "Now, how would you like to criticize my violin playing? I have just learned a new tune."

"Go ahead."

Pawlo went to the closet where his violin was stored and played *Moonlight on the Rhine*, which was a popular tune that year. After listening for a while Erin said, "That was fine but not your style. Why don't you try something else?"

Pawlo played the *Merry Widow Waltz* and after he was finished Erin said, "That's better."

"This is the tune I have asked Mike Sokolosky, the man I bought the violin from when we were both incarcerated at the Brandon Concentration Camp, to play at our wedding."

"I'm certain people at our wedding will enjoy his playing if he plays as well as you do."

Moscow, Russia – November 1917

On the day that Erin and Little Patricia moved in with Pawlo disintegration of the Russian armies progressed steadily, as soldiers deserted their units in great numbers. Excited by all kinds of agitators the Russian soldiers, who were mostly peasants, were in a great hurry to get home and take part in the promised division of the estates of nobility. This had been an old dream of Russian peasantry. On their way home armed gangs of deserters plundered large estates in the regions adjacent to the front murdering their owners, burning down homes and destroying historical places.

On November 6, 1917 the Bolsheviks under Lenin, overthrew the Coalition government and seized power. The destruction of the Old Imperial Army having already been accomplished the Bolsheviks were anxious to end the war with the Central Powers.

On December 15th Lenin and Leon Trotsky signed an armistice and on December 23 peace negotiations broke down because the Bolsheviks would not agree to give up Poland or any western territories to Germany. The Germans resumed their advances and the Bolsheviks agreed to resume negotiations. On March 3 the Treaty of Brest Litovsk was signed. Under the terms of the treaty Russia lost Poland, Ukraine, Finland, Latvia, Estonia and Lithuania.

Some German armies were to occupy all these territories except Finland until the end of the war against the Western Allies. Germany had control of the rich resources of Ukraine, affected much of the effect of the British naval blockade against the Central Powers.

CHAPTER FIFTEEN

As 1917 was nearing an end Pawlo and Erin weren't married but living together. While Little Patricia was playing on the floor her parents were sitting on a couch discussing soldiers in Montreal who did not obey the conscription call.

"An attempt was made to take them by force. The people fought back and there was rioting," Erin said.

"The war seems to be going on and on," Pawlo continued. "Nobody seems to be winning but men are being killed on both sides, crippled and driven mad. And at home Mancan is making less money on pyrohy and holubtsi and people are asking to buy on credit."

"I detect that too," Erin said over a cup of coffee.

"Mancan employees and their families are quite happy, however. That is why they don't belong to a union though I sympathize with what unions are attempting to do." Pawlo said.

"Be truthful with me. Do you belong to a political party?" Erin then asked.

"I would be walking a thin line if I did. There are Conservatives and Liberals but most Ukrainians don't understand what they stand for except that the wealthy belong to them. There are Ukrainian and labor oriented unions and even Jimmy McKernan has joined the Social Democratic Party. As far as I'm concerned it is best we do not join a political party at this time but be observers of human behavior and the free-enterprise system."

A day after Pawlo and Erin had their discussion the government passed another order-in-council. It stated: "Every male person residing in the Dominion of Canada shall be regularly engaged in some useful occupation. If a male person is found by a policeman and a judge not to be usefully occupied the person shall be fined $1000 or sent to jail for a period of six months."

"There are so many laws it's impossible to follow them," Erin said. "And since it's illegal to now criticize Cabinet Ministers people can't complain about food prices, they are horrific."

"Isn't that true? You would think everyone would want to become a Mancan distributor."

There is some good news however."
"What is that?"
"Women have been granted the right to vote in a federal election."

"And now that women are allowed to vote it's their job to purify the politicians." Pawlo said with a hearty laugh, glad that women had the right to vote. "Do you think we will have a woman prime minister in Canada?"
"Eventually England and Canada will have one, but that's decades down the road." Erin said.
That year Pawlo and Erin invited Margaret and Jimmy McKernan to spend Holy Eve and Christmas with them. Christmas was a religious holiday, which the family gave thanks to the birth of Jesus. It was a time Pawlo and Erin along with their guests gave thanks for the success of Mancan and the harvest of the farmers and prayed for future prosperity.
Celebrations for Christmas began Christmas Eve as Little Patricia sat at a window watching for the first evening star to appear. The star represented the star of Bethlehem. When Little Patricia said, "There it is," Pawlo knew it was time to begin the celebration with a meal.

Little Patricia of course, was pleased that she had spotted the star – it meant good fortune during the next year. Perhaps her parents would get her a doll or a stuffed teddy bear from the Mancan catalogue.

Before the table was set for the feast that included twelve meatless and milkless dishes, symbolic of the twelve disciples of the Last Supper, Pawlo went outside and brought in some hay spreading it under the table. The hay represented the manger where Jesus was born. And then Pawlo brought in a sheaf of wheat and with the help of Patricia placed the sheaf in the corner of the dining room. The sheaf symbolized the gathering of a family. Next, three loaves of round bread were placed on the table with a burning candle by the side. The loaves represented the Holy Trinity and the candle the star of Bethlehem.
As they ate Pawlo told Little Patricia Christmas legends with a dog called Seerko and a wolf. The story was about a farm dog that serves his master well, but made a deal with the wolf to kidnap the master's child. When Pawlo finished telling the story Little Patricia laughed until it was time to go to bed.

Jimmy volunteered to baby sit the child until Pawlo, Erin and Margaret returned home from attending midnight mass where at St. Basil's church; Father Patrushka welcomed them and other members of the congregation.

Winnipeg - New Year's Eve - 1918

On New Year's Eve as 1918 was brought in, Pawlo and Erin celebrated again. This time they went to the Ukrainian Hall where their wedding would take place later, and attended a costume ball. Pawlo dressed himself to look like a goat and Erin like a Gypsy. In their costumes they danced until midnight enjoying themselves when a young boy distributed wheat to those present.

"This according to custom will bring prosperity to the New Year," Pawlo said to Erin and joined everyone in the hall to sing traditional Ukrainian songs. Erin wasn't bored a bit.

When There Is Peace in the Family was a popular song at the time and Pawlo sang it interspersing each chorus with a kiss on Erin's cheek. When the singing ended a supper of Ukrainian food was served. Of course there was plenty of pyrohy and holubsti.

After the supper they danced again. And when Erin said, "Whew, I'm exhausted," Pawlo and Erin went home and crawled into bed.

.

Winnipeg – January 1918

As 1918 began the Industrial Workers of the World became an important minority in the United States labor and political scene. The movement was first slow to spread in Canada. The more militant Industrial Workers of the World became the object of anti-sabotage and anti-sedition laws in United States.
It came under a new name One Big Union. As One Big Union, it endorsed a nation-wide alliance of all workers regardless of trades to confront big business.

This was the year the One Big Union and its radical wing was challenging the Trades and Labor Congress in Winnipeg, Northern Ontario and Western Canada. Strikes in the coalfields, mines and lumber camps became almost a common place and so did for the first time Marxist literature and oratory.
The political arm of the Industrial Workers of the World and the One Big Union, the Socialist Democratic Party of Canada, set forth its aims.

In a speech to a group of civic workers in Winnipeg, Jimmy McKernan said, "Our aim is to educate workers of Canada to a conscious of their class position in society, their economic servitude to owners of capital, to seize the reins of government and to transfer all capalistic property into collective property of the working class."

Pawlo and Erin could not believe Jimmy McKernan had gone so radical and distributing pamphlets that assailed not only the sacred cause but also its two most sacred symbols – the Christian Church and the Canadian soldier.

By an order-in-council on October 25 all newspapers in foreign languages were banned. There were additional orders-in-council that led Pawlo to say, "Almost everything in Canada seems illegal."

"Even to get married?" Erin asked as she burst into laughter.

"Don't laugh," Pawlo said, "That too."

Pawlo then explained how an acquaintance of his went downtown but didn't take along his marriage certificate and said, "Police arrested and interrogated the man until he could produce his exemption from conscription."

As the year progressed, the war hysteria culminated with still another order-in-council that forbade strikes and lockouts for the duration of the year. The punishment was a fine of $1000 or six months imprisonment plus drafting the man if he was of military age. It was the same time the One Big Union accepted Karl Marx's concept of the class struggle as a basic tenant, and saw the general strike as the most effective weapon available to the workingman and forecast that a coast-to-coast strike would begin soon. To achieve this goal some of the OBU organizers, who were also Mancan distributors, even traveled by train from one city to another.

"I hear the coal miners are about to strike in Drumheller, Alberta," Erin said.

"I hear that too and that a machine gun has been set up at the mine to prevent the United Workers of America from signing members."

"You know something else?" Erin said.

"What?"

"There's a flu epidemic in Europe."

In Winnipeg there were Ukrainians who were involved in union activities but many were arguing among themselves about an Independent Ukraine.

Some opposed it because it wasn't independent, having been created by the Germans.

While the drama was played out Bishop Budka was already arrested for sedition but released almost immediately. There was a rebellion within his church, which was not connected with his arrest, but the setting of an independent Ukraine. This split among Ukrainians accompanied by charges that the Bishop was forcing assimilation and colluding with Roman Catholics.

Erin kept a record of how may Ukrainians were interned in concentration camps and said she was thankful that Pawlo had been released but expressed concern there were still over 2000 "enemy aliens" interned and 79,000 on parole with Pawlo one of them.

"While I'm free I'm concerned too," Pawlo said and then when another order-in-council was passed on September 18, 1918 to include Russians, Fins and Russian Ukrainians as "enemy aliens" and any one of these who were sixteen had to register with police, he said, "Watch. Still another order-in-council will be passed banning political, fraternal and industrial organizations."

And they were, including the Industrial Workers of the World and the Social Democratic Party that Jimmy McKernan had joined earlier and led by Matthew Popowitch. McKernan was so impressed when he met Popowitch at a gathering to honor the birth date of poet Taras Shevechenko and Popowitch told an audience, "I'm confident that the workers and peasants, our class brothers, will not stop seeking a better life. Now that the tsarist aristocracy is cracked and Nicholas abdicated, the people in Russia will go on forming a provisional government by working people and thus forward to socialism."

World War 1 – April 1918

When World War 1 broke out the history of the aeroplane, inaugurated by the Wright brothers in 1903, spanned a mere eleven years. Most European nations had a few military planes but generally admirals and generals were uniformly skeptical of their usefulness in combat, at most conceding that they may by employed for scouting enemy lines.

The lack of enthusiasm is easily understood. The aircraft of the day were cumbersome, flimsy affairs held together by baling wire. Every flight was an adventure almost as apt to end in a crash as in a safe landing. Engines could crank up no more than 100 horsepower and maximum speeds ranging from 60 to 80 miles an hour, which was about as long as they could stay in the air without landing to refuel. At first none was equipped with armament of any kind.

Canada had no air force of its own, never the less 25,000 became involved in the war in the skies by enlisting in the British Royal Flying Corps and Peter Black (Petro Czorny) was one of the first to join. Black was described as a Canuck in the Flying Corps although he wasn't a Canadian by Canadian standard. As a matter of fact, he didn't know what his status was as he had come to Canada from a province of the Austro-Hungarian Empire called Galicia, as he had escaped from the Brandon Concentration Camp for enemy aliens because of his Ukrainian heritage.

When Black enlisted he simply told the truth and the recruiter in London accepted him for what he was.

The recruiter didn't mind that at the time of the recruitment Peter Black changed his name from Petro Czorny.

"It sounds like an English name," the recruiter said at the time.

Since the development of the aeroplane was so recent there was no history of aerial combat. In this case Peter Black did not suffer from lack of experience. He somehow seemed to be born in a cockpit, as if dueling in the air came naturally to him. As the war continued, Canada could boast having more than her share of flying aces and Peter Black became one of them.

During the first months of hostilities, pilots of opposing armies flew their faltering Bleriots, Farmans and Rumplers on reconnaissance missions over enemy lines with neither the inclination nor equipment to attack one another. Before long, however, they began to devise ways of locking horns in the sky. Some carried rifles, pistols and shotguns. Others threw bricks of lengths of rusty chain in an attempt to foul opposing propellers. A few dangled lead weights on a long wire for the same purpose. In time that was overcome and even machine guns were used.

When this was done the first true fighter planes took to the skies over the Western Front and the area of flying aces was on hand. Germany had several aces also including Ernst Uvet, Max Immeomann and others but the most famous by far was a Prussian nobleman, Baron Manfred von Richthofen, known as the Red Baron or Red Knight. Richthofen flew a bright colored Fokker triplane at the head of his notorious Flying Cross and was credited with 80 victories – the most recorded by any flier on either side.

The Red Baron finally met his end on April 21, 1918 being shot down and the crashing of his death near the Bray-Corbie road behind the British lines. Moments before he plunged to the ground Richtofen was on the tail of a young Canadian pilot, Lieutenant Wilfred "Mop" May. Behind the German ace was another Canadian pilot, Captain Roy Brown, flying a Sopwith Camel. Brown fired several bursts and then watched Richthofen fall away in a deadly spin.

War zone – October 1918

Peter Black was never lucky enough to fly a single seater fighter; instead his career was spent as a pilot of a slow, awkward Armstrong Whtworth FK 8, an observation aircraft. But that did not stop him from attacking Zeppllines, enemy airstrips and German planes that came within machine gun range. In most of these forays Peter Black's gunner was an Englishman who already had won the Military Cross.

On October 27, 1918 Peter Black and his gunner were 500 feet in the air when their plane was attacked by eight German Fokker fighters coming from all directions.

"I'll handle this," the gunner said and fired away.

Again and again Peter Black and his gunner fought off the attackers shooting down three of them.

"That's for Margaret!" Peter shouted to the gunner. "Hold on, we'll get more! Here we go!"

"We are outnumbered!" the gunner shouted back and soon their FK-8 was riddled with bullet holes and so were Peter Black and the gunner.

Peter Black had a slug slam into his leg, another pierced a muscle in his other leg and a third bullet shattered an elbow.

Peter Black was bleeding from his wounds but not only did he manage to keep his plane in the air but continued to press the attack as still more German planes were shot down. Seeing the German planes spin towards the ground Peter Black hollered, "Excellent, a job well done! These planes I'll dedicate to our Conservative MP in Winnipeg Henry Windsor and his son, John,"
As soon as he said those words flames shot back from his planes engine and the petrol tank exploded. Peter Black realized he was in real trouble. The gunner, severely hurt, propped himself and kept on firing his machine gun. Flames kept on shooting from the engine cowling, enveloping the cockpit that left a curling trail of black smoke across the sky as the plane came back to the sullen earth.
"We are going to die!" the gunner cried out but that was not the case as the plane crashed in No Man's Land, not far from the British and Canadian trenches as the Germans kept on firing.

Peter Black, alias Petro Czorny, hair singed, uniform smoldering, weak from loss of blood, succeeded in hauling his gunner from the burning plane. Then encouraged by the nearby Canadian and British soldiers, and protected by covering fire, Peter Black dragged his gunner from shell-hole to shell-hole until they at last reached security of the friendly frontlines.

One of the first to greet Peter Black was John Windsor from Winnipeg. The young Windsor was young and cocky. Upon realizing the pilot he was talking to was Petro Czorny, he exclaimed, "Petro! What are you doing in that plane? I thought you were shot while escaping from the Brandon Concentration Camp."

"I escaped but wasn't killed. It was only a moment ago that I thought about death," Petro answered.

"Wait until my father hears about this," the young Windsor continued and asked, "Are you and Margaret still friends?"

"More than friends, we plan to marry as soon as the war is over."

After saying those words Peter Black collapsed from exhaustion in the young Windsor's arms.

"And he's not even a Canadian," the young Windsor said to the solder next to him, "Petro Czorny was fighting to save me from being killed by the Germans. Dad and I were so mean to him."

It had to take a battlefield for John Windsor to realize that Peter Black and Ukrainians like him were human beings and bled like an Anglo Saxon.

A short time later Peter Black and the gunner were taken to receive medical attention.

At the same time Peter Black had his battle with the Germans in the air those on the ground were in retreat on the front lines and her allies were defeated one by one.

 The whole Austrian-Hungarian Empire was in a state of collapse and November 3 surrendered.

German Surrender – September 8, 1918

On September 8, 1918 a bleak gray day with low slumber clouds and threat of snow in the air French Field Marshal Foch received a German Armistice Commission in a coach of his special train, on a siding near the forest of Compregne.

A coal fire hissed and flared against the external cold and chill of formalities of military and diplomatic protocol. In the early morning of November 11th Germany surrendered and at precisely at 11:00 a.m. the same morning, the guns stopped their firing and all hostilities cased. When that moment arrived, Peter was in a London hospital recovering from his wounds he received when his plane was shot down. With the war over the World and Winnipeg began to celebrate. "Damn it," Peter said to a nurse by his bedside. "I wish Margaret was with me to enjoy this moment in history,"

"If I were you I wouldn't worry. In another several weeks she will be able too. I have just been told by your doctor that your injuries are not that serious that you can be transferred to Winnipeg."

Winnipeg – November 11, 1918

Pawlo was in the Mancan building where employees were making pyrohy and holubtsi when the news of the Armistice reached Winnipeg. It was 3:00 p. m. when he told his employees, "Stop all work! Go and celebrate!"

Then directing his remarks to Mike Sokolosky, Pawlo went on, "This is a moment in history far greater important when serfdom was abolished in Ukraine in 1848 by Ferdinand 1 of Austria.

Take rest of day off, each one of you."
All over Winnipeg, factory whistles blew, church bells pealed, fire department sirens wailed. Work came to a complete stop. Some impromptu parades clogged the streets. Thousands laughed, cheered, shouted, sang patriotic songs and some even dragged a replica of the German Kaiser behind their cars.

While the World War may have ended, a civil one broke out in Ireland. The question was whether the country should be a Free State within the British Commonwealth, or a completely independent nation. Families were divided, and friend was pitted against friend. Property was destroyed and blood was shed.

Winnipeg – November 1918

In Canada, when the celebration calmed down, the soldiers began returning home.

After four years of fighting some came back blind, some lacking arms and legs, some with their minds destroyed, many doomed to spend the rest of their lives in veterans' hospitals from Halifax to Victoria.

When they came back to was certainly a Canada that changed in many ways. The immediate legacy of the war, apart from casualties, included rampant inflation, widespread unemployment and a shortage of adequate housing.

Peter Black, after he was transferred from London to the Winnipeg General Hospital, and veterans like him, were surprised by the number of changes in Winnipeg. One was a dramatic increase in the number of cars. Bars and saloons were gone and bootleggers prevalent. Soldiers who got home early witnessed some results of the emancipation women had received during the war – including the right to vote, and increased freedom to dress as they saw fit. A few women, and not just streetwalkers, actually smoked a cigarette in public. One of these women was Margaret Carpenter who Peter Black was courting.

It was the same time the war brought about great advances in technology to radios, and a few pioneer stations in United States were broadcasting for several hours of music each day.
In Canada the Marconi Wireless Telegraph Company was offering receiver parts for sale.

When Pawlo complained about the deteriorating economic conditions, Erin said to him, "Be patient. Calm down. Things are bound to get better for Mancan." But they didn't in the immediate future even with Peter Black's help.
In their personal lives, Pawlo and Erin experienced trouble too, particularly when Dr. Kozak said to them, "Little Patricia has a cough that is difficult to get rid of."
Eventually Little Patricia's coughing became more frequent, but she wasn't the only one as a virulent flu struck not only Europe but also rest of the world and medical authorities were powerless to keep the disease from spreading. People turned in desperation to a bizarre variety of cures and preventative. Everyone stopped shaking hands, they wore masks while outdoors, they did not spit and some stopped kissing.

Many used poultices; others drank concoctions of warm milk, ginger, soda, sugar and black pepper.

"Why I stay healthy, I guess, is because I eat cloves of garlic and drink chokecherry wine," Pawlo said to Dr. Kozak when questioned about his health. "To bad that due to the prohibition all saloons in Winnipeg are closed and there is no vodka available."

No remedy really worked and the epidemic continued to spread its inexorable rampage, which forced Little Patricia to be taken to the Winnipeg General Hospital. This, despite, that chemists, at Mancan worked day and night attempting to discover a medicine to cure the flu.

A week later, Little Patricia was still lying in bed in the children's ward with a respirator and coughing violently. Her eyes were bleary and her breathing heavy. Erin tried to comfort her daughter by placing an additional blanket on top of her when Dr. Kozak stepped into the room.

"Little Patricia is coughing violently." Pawlo said to Dr. Kozak.

"She is a sick child and the only one God gave us," Erin said then turning to Pawlo continued," We better call Father Patrushka to come and baptize her."

"I have already sent a message with a courier. He should be here any moment."

Dr. Kozak gave Little Patricia some medicine and after putting the bottle away said, "It's bronchitis of the severest kind spreading like a prairie fire throughout the world. I'm afraid…"

Pawlo tried to say something but his lips froze. It was the worst feeling he had experienced all his life, a child dying. At that moment Father Patrushka entered the room with the sacraments and after consulting with Dr. Kozak, Pawlo and Erin said, "Pawlo and Erin you should pray as in a short while Little Patricia will be in heaven."

The kindly priest first baptized Little Patricia and then gave her the last rites – the sacrament of Extreme Unction.

Pawlo and Erin saw tears on Father Patrushka's cheeks and felt tears of sadness on their own faces as in union they prayed, "In the name of the Father, the son and the Holy Ghost…."

As soon as Dr. Kozak saw the tears he said to Father Patrushka, Pawlo and Erin, "It's all right to cry. Even Jesus wept at a funeral of a friend."

After several minutes Little Patricia lapsed into unconsciousness, her fever rose and her lungs congested. Even Dr. Kozak could not save the child and like 65,000 other Canadians was the victim of the epidemic and pronounced dead.

Russia – May 1919

On the day of the funeral for Little Patricia it was bitterly cold in Winnipeg and winds gusted to fifty miles an hour building snowdrifts three feet deep. When the funeral was over and everyone leaving the cemetery Pawlo walked up to Henry Windsor and wanted to know what an Expeditionary of Canadian troops was doing in Siberia since the war was over and Russia had opted out and signed a treaty with the Central Powers. Windsor replied as he was about to climb into his car, "A brigade of Canadian artillery is in Archangel. The brigade arrived there two months before the Armistice was signed.

There are about 4000 Allied troops in Vladivostock and other contingents around Murmansk. In all there are one-half million troops in Russia."

Windsor said the expeditionary force intended to help White Russians battle the Red Army following the revolution and the overthrow and execution of Czar Nicholas. Canadian troops joined soldiers from Britain, France, United States and Japan and had a very specific purpose.
They were to prevent their ally, Russia, from falling under the control of the Bolsheviks, who it was feared, would capitulate and sign a peace treaty with Germany.

The Canadian soldiers finally returned to Canada after the government began to listen to public clamor to bring them home. The soldiers came back without firing a shot. By the end of 1919, most of the Allied troops had withdrawn as well. After some initial success in aiding White Russian forces, the tide turned and the Reds able to seal victory.
"But I thought the war was over," Pawlo said. In reply Windsor said, "About Canadian soldiers in Siberia, what you don't know, doesn't matter."

"It hurts me that the Canadian government has transferred 1843 men, members of the North West Mounted Police, six officers and 181 horses from Winnipeg to Russia and only a handful of politicians know it. Whom are they supposed to be fighting?" Pawlo asked.

"The Red Army."

"What for?"

"So that you can have an Independent Ukraine and move the hell out of Canada."

Ottawa – May 15, 1919

Windsor wasn't so forceful several months later when in the Parliament Buildings in Ottawa Lieutenant Peter Black received a citation for his heroics as a pilot during the war from the Governor General of Canada, Duke of Devonshire. Either through coincidence or through special aptitude, Canadians including Peter Black created a remarkable record. The most famous of these of course was Billy Bishop, who destroyed 77 enemy planes, including five on his last day over Germany,

Another young pilot, Billy Barker, won the Military Cross with two bars, the Distinguished Service Order and the Victoria Cross. Eighteen year old Alan McLeod won the Victoria Cross and Lieutenant Peter Black wasn't far behind winning a citation that read: "Set upon at 500 feet above earth with eight enemy machines Lieutenant Peter Black so maneuvered his aeroplane that his gunner was able to shoot down three of the assailants. Although wounded in five places himself, when his petrol tank was set on fire he continued to control it so his gunner could continue the battle with the machine gun and shoot down two more.

Then when Lieutenant Peter Black brought his burning machine to earth in No Man's Land and before dropping from loss of blood, he saved the life of his gallant gunner, and this while under fire by the Germans." Following the presentation by the Governor General a reporter asked Peter Black about the citation.

"I would like to thank the awards committee. Indeed winning the citation is a great honor."

"Great enough to live in Canada permanently?"

"Great enough to marry my fiancée, Margaret Carpenter, and become a Canadian." Peter Black said and went on, "I'm certain my changing the surname from Czorny to Black did not influence the awards committee.

"I'm also certain the committee took into consideration that I had escaped from the Brandon Concentration Camp as an alien and an enemy of Canada because of my Ukrainian heritage."

"Well, do you now consider yourself as an alien?" the reporter continued to probe.

"Only Canadian Anglo Saxons do. I'm certain with time that will change too."

As Peter Black was speaking to the reporter he picked up a copy of the *Ottawa Citizen* newspaper, which described Canadian air force heroes. On a page beside an article describing Peter Black's citation, he noticed an advertisement next to it that read: "Dr. Chases Nerve Food for All Shell Shocked Soldiers."

The reporter then touched Peter Black on the shoulder and said, "Congratulations on winning the citation and your forthcoming marriage to Margaret Carpenter but tell me sir, have you heard the news that broke in Winnipeg today?"

"What news?"

`There`s a strike. ``

"I'm not surprised. I do hope however, that the strike is over by the time Margaret and I, and Pawlo and Erin get married. Our wedding date and plans have already been arranged."

CHAPTER FIFTEEN

Winnipeg – May, 1919

Ever since the Armistice was signed, Mancan products kept selling despite economic conditions beginning to decline in Winnipeg. Prices for all commodities began to rise while the size of the underpaid force increased. The Trades and Labor Council began to flex its muscle while those who were trying to promote the One Big Union were getting more militant. The farmers weren't happy either. The earlier image of Ukrainian immigrants as being easy prey to political corruption had on occasion given way to the image that the immigrant was a dangerous revolutionary. There were troublesome issues pressing for settlement as the troops came marching home. A new and more complicated war awaited them in their civil affairs – a class war. For most part the "Winnipeg Revolutionaries" as they were called then, took their cases and catechism second hand. Their heroes were Keir Hardy, Ramsay McDonald, Robert Owen and Sidney Webb from Great Britain; Lenin and Trotsky from Russia; Eugene Debs, Emma Goldman and Mother Jones from United States.

They borrowed their martyrs, the Joe Hills and Tom Mooney's, and their demons, the Rockefellers, Morgan's, Schwab's, DuPont's and Armour's, wealthy industrialists in United States.

They borrowed their plan of actions from what appeared to be a freshly surging fountainhead of the Industrial Workers of the World.

Bargaining had to be done industry wide, the separate unions of the Central Metal Trades Council insisted. All the chief employers were willing to bargain collectively but only with their employees. Building-Trade workers had struck on the same day on a straight question of wages. Within a week 52 other unions voted to walk out in sympathy. On May 12 the Trades and Labor Council, the local body of the Congress, beat the One Big Union to the punch and issued the long awaited decree: A general strike was called all organizations affiliated with the Council.

Winnipeg-May 15, 1919 – City Strike

Overnight, Canada's third largest city lay half paralyzed and stagnant.

The streetcars stopped running and but a handful of postmen walked their beats. Cooks, waiters, bakers and clerks went on strike. So were teamsters, truck drivers, plumbers, carpenters, street cleaners and even the sanitation men, which included Jimmy McKernan.

So were the telephone operators, firemen, elevator operators, butchers, milkmen icemen, breadmen; many of which were part-time Mancan distributors.

Employees of the waterworks left only enough crews on duty to keep the pressure at 30 pounds – just sufficient for the water to reach the second stories.

Police voted to strike but remained on duty at the urging and "permission" of the Strike Committee, which set up headquarters to look over the affairs of the city in the four-story headquarters of the Labor Temple,

It poured out a stream of decrees and regulations that led Windsor to comment, "I'm not going to stand for this. Not since the reign of Louis X1V has the civil power been interfered so cavalierly in so many of the ordinary details of day-to-day life in Canada."

Pawlo Bilyi and Peter Black expressed concern too when the Mancan General Store they purchased from Nathan Tarnoff was ordered to close down by the Trades and Labor Council executive.

"This is without a doubt a monopoly," Peter Black said to the union leaders. "People need bread and milk to live. Furthermore, none of our employees belong to a union so why are you shutting us down?"

Telegraph companies were permitted to send dispatches to other parts of Canada and United States but as Pawlo and Peter found out when they wanted to communicate with Mancan distributors, the copy had to be cleared by a four-man board of censors.

As soon as the store was closed down, it was ordered to stay open. The store could sell milk, bread, pyrohy, holubtsi but not ice cream. Ice cream was classed as unproleterian luxury and remained under ban.

Several days later Pawlo and Peter were told that they could sell only to customers wearing union badges and were warned that if their employees made any derogatory remarks to the strikers the store would be closed again.

Sympathy strike broke out in other cities but nowhere was the terror complete or general as in Winnipeg.

"The whole country is heading for anarchy!" Windsor said to Mayor Gray and cried out to Prime Minister Borden by long distance telephone saying, "The forces of law must assert itself."

Immediately the Prime Minister notified the Postal Minister who phoned Windsor back and said, "The postmen who walked out have done so without justification and I remind those who stayed on the job that the government is standing absolutely behind them."

Windsor, a veteran politician that he was, and the Mayor were also assured by other cabinet ministers that modest reinforcements would be added to the city's military and the North West Mounted Police garrison and when time came were kept out of sight in their barracks.

It was ten days before Mayor Gray and City Council could bring itself to pass a resolution against sympathy strikes by civic employees, and even then the vote was close.

Mayor Gray in a statement assured the citizens that they could count on having water, milk, basic foodstuffs, and fire and public protection.

"We are securing these rights by sufferance of some other authority than the constituted authority of city government," the Mayor said to those who came to City Hall with their complaints."

The first rally organized against the strikers' dictatorship came from a group of affluent Anglophone capitalists who took the name of Citizens Committee and with 1000 members set up headquarters in the Board of Trade building.

"We'll show those Communists who is running the City," the Mayor said to Windsor and ultimately the committee grew to 10,000 and offered volunteer firemen, police and emergency help in other public utilities. Heartened by its support, the Mayor overcame a feeling of helplessness and made another declaration: "The constituted authorities are determined to stamp out the Bolsheviks or the Red element in our city. Winnipeg is open; all businesses may go ahead as in the past.

No one section of the public has the right to dictate food terms to any other section of the public. This principle will be strictly adhered by the constituted authorities."

A short time after Mayor Gray said those words, the strike-bound newspapers mustered enough pressmen to start putting out abbreviated editions again and one of them, the Free Press, set up a radio station on its building roof and assured the world, "The city of Winnipeg is still functioning. There has been no violence."

Many of the unofficial spur-of-the-moment, non-union strikers, who had outnumbered the official union strikers by about 18,000 to 12,000, began to drift to their jobs. The sound of delivery horses was heard again on city streets.

Scores of Small stores followed the example of the Big stores. Soon other retail stores followed and everything seemed normal. But when Pawlo saw two Federal cabinet ministers roam the streets of Winnipeg he said to Peter Black, "The city is in trouble"

"If that is the case should we postpone our wedding?" Pawlo asked.

"Definitely not, I think, however, the ministers will order all Federal employees back to work."

And they did.

The minister of Labor ordered postmen to go back to work while the Minister of the Interior urged the populace to "Stay firm."

Winnipeg – May 20, 1919

A day after the Minister said those words Pawlo Bily1 and Petro Czorny officially changed their names to Paul White and Peter Black. The following Saturday they married Erin and Margaret Carpenter. The wedding took place in St. Basils Greek Catholic Church with Father Patrushka performing the ceremony.

The senior Windsor and his son John, stayed only for the church service and to give the brides away and then, because of an important meeting pertaining to what was happening in Winnipeg, the Senior Windsor took a train bound for Ottawa.

Both Erin and Margaret wore a white dress and a veil but they had no bridesmaids.

They wore metallic colored shoes and carried a bouquet of flowers. Paul White and Peter Black wore dark colored suits with a rose in the lapel.

The most important part of the wedding was a religious ceremony.

The two couples knelt in front of the altar on an embroidered runner when Father Patrushka gave them the sacraments of communion and marriage. Each bride and groom was crowned with a wreath, a symbol that they would wear in Heaven. After the ceremony the crowns were to be framed and hang in their bedrooms as a reminder of the sacredness of the wedding.

After the couples were married and each said, "I do," Father Patrushka looked up and said, "Paul White, Peter Black, Erin and Margaret Carpenter, this is the first marriage between Anglophones and Ukrainians that I have performed and the grooms have legally changed their names to accommodate their wives. Your lives have just begun in the holy sacrament of Matrimony. This is a culmination of knowing each other for a long time and I'm touched by the commitment you have promised each other.

Most in this room make mistakes and can learn from others' errors, successes, struggles and failures. As you know we struggle against injustices, dreamed of freedom and democracy and a better economic order."

Next, picking up a manuscript Father Patrushka kept hidden under the altar cloth, congratulated the blind Margaret for writing a book of short stories and a drama about Ukrainian women in Winnipeg.
Father Patrushka went on, "The play, entitled *Carolina Finds a Husband* will be premiered at the Walker Theatre next December and her book, A Basketful of Ukrainian Short Stories will be published about the same time by a publisher in Chicago."

The wedding reception took place at the Ukrainian National Hall that same evening and partying lasted three days. Among those attending were Erin and Margaret's parents, Sean and Anne Carpenter, who arrived from Cork, Ireland for the occasion. Also present were Paul White's parents and Peter Black's father who had applied as immigrants to Canada.

'It was love at first sight," Patricia Windsor said to Sean Carpenter to which he replied, "Look, love doesn't need a second language." The weather was superb. A glorious June day smiled on the world and all around the hall wagons and buggies were neatly parked and bicycles rested against the walls of the hall and nearby trees.

A crowd of people in its Sunday best was inside the hall chattering gaily. The strike that the Trades and Labor Congress called was on the minds of many of the guests but at the moment Paul and Erin. Peter and Margaret were centre stage.

The latest styles of clothes mingled with costumes from Galicia. English speaking women and buxom Ukrainian girls in the same crowd strutted about, all waiting for the brides and grooms, and when they did come, there were shouts, "There they are!"

Then the crowd waited for Father Patrushka and when he showed up they gave him a rousing, "Slava Inusu Khrysti!" intermingled with "Good evening, Father," just as loud as when the brides and grooms were greeted. Within an hour the hall was jammed with people, many standing outside and looking in through the windows.

"Assimilation," Patricia said to Jimmy McKernan as they watched the two married couples cuddle up to each other and from time to time express their secret desires, feelings and hopes for the future. The guests, notwithstanding from different ethnic origins, mingled well in company, conversed with each other and shared in the food and drink which was set out on a table.

After the meal, at which Father Patrushka said grace, and included pyrohy and holubtsi came the strains of a violin, a waltz tune, played by Mike Sokolosky.

As soon as they heard the sound of the violin playing, they newly wed took to dance floor and then other couples joined in.

"Assimilation," Patricia Windsor said again as her and Jimmy McKernan were dancing but this time Jimmy replied, "Assimilation but perhaps extinction also."

Soon the pace of activity increased as a five-piece band played and everyone was swinging partners and enjoying themselves until daybreak next morning.

The lively English men, some from wealthy families, kept whirling hefty Ukrainian girls until both were on the verge of collapsing from exhaustion.

And the handsome, strapping Ukrainian men took a back seat to no one as they swung away with pretty English-speaking girls on the dance floor. No one seemed to care that Winnipeg strike was on but that was the reason the two newly married couples did not go on a honeymoon. Instead they each purchased a new home in North Winnipeg and moved into it.

The wedding and the strike took place at a time when thousands of returning soldiers saw in the strike their first chance to get back at authorities because they could not find jobs. They were also tired of the authority which they were used to in military service.

The Mayor, the Mounties, the cabinet ministers from Ottawa, Windsor, and all the harassed employers represented all the majors, company commanders and the generals wrapped up in one vulnerable target. And while the officers of the new and fast growing veterans' associations passed resolutions condemning the strike, their members paraded through the streets cheering and upholding it.

Three deputations ranging from 1000 to 3000 marched on the Provincial Building to shout obscenities at the premier of Manitoba. Another procession marched at City Hall to take issue with Mayor Gray, and still another marched up Wellington Crescent where Windsor and the wealthy Anglophones lived, and booed them.

By this time, Mayor Gray, forbade all parades and all but fifteen members of the police were fired, the Police Commission having demanded and failed to get from them a retraction of their first vote in support of the strike.
The hitherto invisible Mounties began patrolling the streets and Special Officers from the Citizen's Committee replaced the municipal force.
The following day, a mob set upon two of the Special Officers at the junction of Portage and Main. The Mounties rode to their rescue with batons flying and the ensuing riot lasted five hours, although no one was seriously hurt.

A week later, and thirty-three days after the walkout had become general; the government in Ottawa had nothing less than a seditious conspiracy.

There were hysterical reports of a Soviet government being set up in Winnipeg and the cabinet ministers; Mayor Gray and Windsor were convinced the revolution had begun. "Is the Union Jack or the Red Flag to fly over Canada?" Windsor asked his Citizen Committee members one morning and during the same afternoon continued, "Money from Moscow is supporting the strike."
There was no proof.

Next day in a theatrical series of early morning arrests, in which fifty Mounties and Special Policemen took part.
A dozen of the most prominent strike leaders were bundled up in automobiles, and rushed to the nearby Federal penitentiary at Stony Mountain. In the next few days more of the alleged conspirators joined them, having been picked up as far apart as Calgary and Montreal.
Of the men jailed in the roundup five were ideally equipped for the role of Bolshevik politics.
They had warty faces and all were known to have been or believed born in Russia. But as the crown set out the preparation of its case an awkward climax happened.

There was hardly any evidence against the five Russians and the case against them had to be dropped which made Windsor angry.

"Fit to be tied," is how Patricia called her husband's conduct.

This left the Department of Justice to press its charges against ten Anglo Saxons, two of them were ordained Christian ministers, two others were aldermen in the city of Winnipeg, one was a member of the Manitoba Legislative Assembly and the other five were labor union leaders of considerable authority and prestige.

Before the trial began news of the arrests spread and touched a final outburst on Saturday, June 21 around City Hall and the Market Square behind it. At the time an announcer at the radio station intoned, "It's twelve-noon. A large crowd is gathering at City Hall and is becoming unruly."   ·

Paul and Erin were in their apartment at the time relaxing. Hearing the announcer on the radio, Erin said, "Paul isn't there something you can do?"

"Up to now there has been no violence," Paul said while looking through a set of binoculars and went on, "But since many Ukrainians are in the crowd maybe I can have some influence."

Paul and Erin each grabbed their jackets and ran toward City Hall where Jimmy McKernan was more visible than most people in the crowd. He was shouting obscenities at Mayor Gray. While he was doing that, a streetcar came clanging along Main Street, and because of the crowd was forced to stop. A pan was pulled out of the streetcar, other demonstrators swarmed aboard, the motormen fled and the few terrified passengers escaped to safety.

Windows were smashed, cushions torn apart, seats ripped out, then flames leaved up and oily black smoke puffed over the scene. Suddenly there was a clatter of hoof beats on the brick pavement coming from the direction of Portage Avenue, and waves of scarlet-khaki Mounties came charging north of Main Street. The mob fell back, shouting defiance, some hurling stones, bricks and bottles.

The mounted policemen swung away with clubs until their horses were stopped by the sheer mass of the demonstrators.

Winnipeg – May 31, 1919

In the midst of the confusion, Mayor Gray read the Riot Act from the steps of City Hall, but not many people could hear what he was saying. The Mounties regrouped and attacked once more, this time brandishing pistols instead of truncheons.

"My God! These are real bullets. The Mounties are shooting to kill," Erin said to Paul when she heard shots fired by policemen. Several dozen demonstrators were trapped in a dead-end street. They were beaten to the ground by police and trampled by horses they were riding on.

A convoy of cars and trucks, loaded with soldiers with fixed bayonets and machine guns, made way through the milling crowd, but by then the fighting was all but over. Soon the strikers and their supporters began to drift away. By nightfall the chief pyrohy and holubtsi maker at Mancan, Mike Sokolosky, who was in the crowd was killed, 91 other people were in jail and another 30 in hospitals.

The spirit of the workers had been crushed by bloodshed and by obvious determination of authorities to use whatever force might be necessary to maintain order.

To all intent the Winnipeg Strike was over and both Paul White and Peter Black called the incident a 'Bloody Saturday'. Several days following the strike Peter Black said to Paul White, "We have to change the system."
"By that you mean?"
"Like distributing Mancan products it has to start from the grass roots. The strikers have failed and all they got was a Commission which will investigate."

As soon as the decade was drawing to a close the British Nationality Act was rescinded. Paul White, Peter Back and their wives became British Subjects and the principal actors who held centre stage since they arrived in Canada were making their exits. Laurier at 78 survived two strokes but died of a third. On the 11th of February 1919, clasping his wife's hands as she sat at his bedside, he whispered, "Cest fini" and closed his eyes for the last time.
Henry Bourassa with thirty-five years of life ahead of him retired to twilight of quiet observation, somehow lost now that he no longer had Sir Wilfred Laurier to provide counterpoint to his opinions.

"He knew that, although I fought him because of differences of principle, I loved him all my life," the publisher of Le Devoir noted sadly on learning of Laurier's death.

Winnipeg – summer 1920

Prime Minister Borden who exhausted his limited strengths, first in directing the war effort and in fighting for, and winning Canada's rights to full partnership in peace settlements at Versailles, announced his desire to retire from public life which he did in the summer of 1920.
Waiting in the wings ere new leaders; William Lyon Mackenzie King, Arthur Meighen and James Woodsworth. And the backdrop would be that of the Roaring Twenties.

The Roaring Twenties was also the theme of another Mancan annual meeting in Winnipeg. It was also a time distributors from throughout Canada and the World were rewarded for their efforts during 1919. The meeting took place in the Board of Trade Auditorium and as co-founders of Mancan Paul White and Peter Black, gave brief messages of encouragement.

Paul White began by saying, "The past year has been a time of economic hardship for many countries and companies. Some had to reluctantly pull back and retrench. Some distributors had to close doors forever. During the 1919 fiscal year Mancan and its distributors however, reported another record-breaking year,"

Peter Black highlighted the financial statement, people and places, and the products that played an important role in Mancan's record-breaking year.

"But what you see here is only the tip of the iceberg," Peter continued. "Behind the record achievement are really important success stories of Mancan, the customers served, the new homes built, education finances, charities and churches supported, and all of the many other experiences of personal growth and fulfillment that have come to pass because of the Mancan business."

Here, Paul took over, "We are blessed with this year's growth and salute Mancan's 100,000 distributors worldwide and the three hundred employees at our plant in Winnipeg. Because of you, we have reasons to believe 1920 will be another outstanding year of progress and achievement.

This was our dream when Peter Black and Paul White were still living in Galicia."
There was thunderous applause and Peter Black next introduced company executives and then called on distributors that achieved the highest level of success and leadership to come onto the stage.

Their everyday tools were anything from an axe, grease paint, law books, mountains, prairies, office buildings, Main Street and Lakeshore Drive. Their special interest was Mancan and together these people from all walks of life and all parts of the world combined into a positive force envied by Henry Windsor and other Anglophone merchants in Winnipeg.

Winnipeg – January, 1921

One of the first things Windsor did once the strike was over was to call a meeting of the Soldiers' Relatives Association and a committee was struck to raise funds for a memorial.

The city had erected a makeshift memorial at the corner of Portage and Main to serve Armistice Day wreath-laying ceremonies in November.

However it was on a piece of property owned by a bank, which decided it, wanted a permanent memorial of its own on the site so the city's memorial had to be removed.

In due time, the bank's eight foot statue arrived. Somewhere, somehow, things for the bank went awry – the bank memorial was a figure of an American soldier.

"What is a Canadian bank doing glorifying an American soldier," Windsor said to Patricia as they were strolling along the street.

"Probably the bank thinks the Americans won the war that the British Empire couldn't do themselves," Patricia replied.

"Nonsense. United States did not enter the war until it was almost over."

Windsor immediately had the committee appoint a board of nationally known artists and architects to judge designs submitted for the memorial and when they were received, Windsor said to the committee chairman. "In order to guarantee impartiality have all identifying marks removed from the models."

The committee governing the contract, worth $25,000, was given wide publicity and 48 designs were received from all parts of

Canada. Despite this imposing array of entries, the judges came to a final decision.

"I agree not only is the model submitted by Emanuel Hahn of Toronto is outstanding, it is one of the finest examples of that type of art," Windsor said when he heard the decision.

The committee's four page accolade in part read: "The board feels that the highest respect is due to the power of this designer exhibits in setting forth this fine idea in carrying out his works on a full scale will develop his thought in still a higher degree."

The ultimate accolade for the design came not from the judges but Hahn's peers. Several of them said upon seeing the design that they agreed with the judges, it was the only possible choice.

Sitting in the living room with his wife, Windsor said, "Hahn? Doesn't that sound like a German name? Can't be, no Hahn would have enough nerve to put in a design for a Canadian cenotaph depicting the sacrifice our soldiers made."

"Probably he's a Belgian or a Hollander," Patricia suggested. "These names sound all alike to me."

"It won't do any harm to find out. Why don't you call the *Free Press* just for fun?"

And when Patricia did make the call, her husband became furious. Emanuel Hahn was of German birth, having come to Canada 38 years before as a boy of seven.

A member of the family of distinguished artists and musicians, he had attended Toronto public schools, eventually studied in Europe and at present was the head of the sculpture department of the Ontario College of Art. Hahn had a wide reputation as a designer of war memorials, no fewer than nine Canadian cities having chosen his work.

With the urging of Windsor, Veteran groups met in special sessions to denounce the sacrilege of having a German design a memorial to Canadian soldiers killed in a war whose country was the main protagonist. "I would be inclined to spit on Hahn's memorial. It is an insult to the Canadian soldiers," Windsor said to the Veterans. "May I suggest the design be restricted to those of British subjects or Canadian birth?"

The Veteran groups passed various resolutions and wrote letters to the newspapers opposing the Hahn design.

Veterans were seconded by the Imperial Daughters of the Empire and perhaps most important of all, the Winnipeg Board of Trade, of which Windsor was an active member. Windsor also attacked the notion that naturalized Canadians should achieve quality in patriotism with natural born citizens.

When some said that Popowitch was not necessarily a good comparison Windsor replied, "To ask a man whom was German born to build such a monument is like asking a relative of a murdered man to accept a memorial by a cousin of the man who committed the murder."

After hearing about the uproar Hahn offered to ease the embarrassment of the committee by withdrawing his design. The gesture was refused but in the end the name Hahn, the German immigrant boy, proved too much for the committee and paid him off with $2500 and called for a second contest.

"This time the eligibility is confined to Canadian citizens born in Canada, the British Empire or in Allied countries," Windsor said and the committee agreed to give it another shot to find the right memorial.

This design provoked a hassle however, with the Royal Architectural Institute when two architects on the original committee resigned to protest. One of them said, "Hahn is the winner and it should remain that way."
The second contest attracted twenty five designs and the judges unveiled their choice as winner of the second go-round. It was an entry by Elizabeth Wyn Wood of Toronto that Windsor agreed with the judges was a remarkable work of art.
"The winning design, in my opinion is remarkable for its heroic proportions and is bound to attract the attention of passersby. It avoids the similarity of some many of our war memorials already erected," Windsor said to Patricia while they were driving a Model T Ford on a Winnipeg street.

More important than providing a winning design of great artistic merit the winner had an authentic Anglo-Saxon name that had a ring to it.
"Elizabeth Wyn Wood. That's a name of British origin," Windsor said and then was piqued that a woman should walk off with first prize in a field that was almost a male monopoly.

"Will you please call the *Free Press* and check out her background," Windsor said to Patricia for the second time, and when she did, discovered Miss Elizabeth Wyn Wood was a recent bride of Emmanuel Hahn. Well, doo-doo hit the fan.

"I can't believe it! Hahn entered the contest under his wife's maiden name!" Windsor exclaimed.

Even the United Veterans Group agreed that the likelihood of two outstanding designers of war memorials were to be found within a single Toronto was too remote a possibility for serious consideration.

"Who believes a twenty three-year-old woman who recently graduated from an art school could produce such a spectacular work of sculpture.Windsor protested.

Unlike the opposition to Emmanuel Hahn, which built slowly, the Wood design grew quickly.

Unlike the first struggle, in which they had a specific issue on which to focus – Hahn's birth in Germany – the opposition to the design had nothing more to go on except Miss Wood's questionable choice of a husband.

"You can hardly reject her entry on the grounds that she's a woman. Can you?" Patricia asked.

"We can."

"How?"

"The War Widows Association says the design does not portray what their sons died for. In fact Miss Wood's design is not a cenotaph at all."

This gave the committee a way out. The design was not a cenotaph. It rejected Miss Wood's entry and sent $500 to cover her expenses and hoped it would get rid of the Hahn's provided there were no more cousins lurching to take part in a third contest.

The committee side-stepped around any such hazard by passing over the second place winner and bestowing what was left of the honor of designing Winnipeg's cenotaph to a local English born architect who was employed by the provincial government.

In order to dampen the uproar Windsor wrote a letter to the local newspapers defending his colleagues attacking Miss Wood's design and praising the final choice of the committee.

In reply Miss Woods wrote a letter to the
same newspapers and wanted one thing
straight. In part the letter read:

"The conditions of the contest, unlike the first
one, made no mention of the word cenotaph
in four pages of instructions the word was not
mentioned once, the words war memorial and
monument, were. At no place was the word
cenotaph implied."

After checking out the conditions Windsor
said, "I agree with what Miss Wood says.
The word cenotaph was not used even once."

"Hearing the comment Patricia replied,
"That's one thing you can't blame on the
Germans or Ukrainians."

Paul White and Peter Black remained active
and visited as many distributors as they could.
It was following a visit to Winnipeg
distributors that Paul White met Windsor on
the corner of Portage and Main and Windsor
stopped, looked and asked White if he would
consider giving a speech to the Winnipeg
Board of Trade.

"I'd be delighted to say something," White
said, and when he did, began with, "Friends.
Today I want to share with you a few
thoughts about Canada, freedom and free
enterprise."

When the Board of Trade members were settled in their places and there was total silence he continued, "I appreciate efforts by governments to solve strikes, unemployment and poverty but I cannot tolerate people who continually hate other people because they are not Anglophones or that continually complain its somebody else's problem.

"I maintain that anyone who puts down another person because he does not speak his language or is his religion isn't of the same political persuasion or color of skin, will never succeed in business.

"I maintain one should be rewarded for the efforts he or she puts into finding employment.

For instance the Mancan Corporation that Peter Black and I co-found has annual sales of over $100-million, 50,000 distributors throughout the world and 300 employed at its Winnipeg factory. We sell $10-million worth of you know what – pyrohy and holubtsi. And we deliver soap and cosmetics and other catalogue products to the customer instead of the customer going to the store for it.

"I realize that many soldiers have returned home from the war and there is high unemployment.

Those who tell you opportunities do exist don't believe them. I happen to know that there is more opportunity with Mancan than ever before."

Near the end of the speech Paul White said, "Some are talking about how good things come from Russia under Communism.
 Well, if that is the case why don't they go there? Anyone is free to leave Canada, but they don't want to go. So let's stop grumbling about foreigners who are living in Winnipeg and how rotten our society is. Let's tell these people how great it is to be a Canadian.
"Just as I stand for our system I stand for my Ukrainian heritage and religious beliefs. Even with the war over, I still see the world as one large concentration camp, which I have some experience with. People are trying to escape from freedoms we enjoy.

You and I should shout about Canada not as Anglophone, Francophone or Ukrainian, German, Polish or Chinese but support each other, respect each other, and sell Canada and the freedoms we enjoy.

I'm asking you to sell Canada regardless of your color, race, religious or economic station. Let's march together as a united people building a great nation. To quote our former prime minister, Sir Wilfred Laurier the 'Twentieth century belongs to Canada'." There was a tumultuous applause by the Board of Trade members. Even Henry Windsor stood up and applauded.

Chicago – December, 1921

Several days after Paul White spoke to the Winnipeg Board of Trade members he, Erin, Peter Black and his wife Margaret, traveled to Chicago where they discussed with Margaret's publisher the upcoming release of her *A Basketful of Ukrainian Short Stories.*

EPILOGUE

Winnipeg – December, 1921

Three days after returning to Winnipeg the White's and Black's drove to the Walker Theatre to attend the premier of Margaret's play, *Carolina Catches a Husband,* that dealt with an Irish woman marrying a Ukrainian. Basically it was Margaret's own autobiography filled with anecdotes and humor. Margaret wore a striking red dress with a black wool coat for the occasion and looked wonderful.

Margaret almost trembled as she heard bursts of applause throughout the production. She was excited about the play that featured local actors and the possibility it could end up on Broadway.

When Margaret woke up next morning, she found that newspaper literary critics were just praiseworthy of the play as the audience the night before. A critic for the *Free Press* wrote in his review: "The plot of Mrs. Black's drama twists and turns as an incredible humorous story unfolds to the thrills and delight of the audience

This blind Canadian woman is an upcoming writer, influenced by the works of James Joyce, George Bernard Shaw and William Butler Yeats."

The following day, a reporter from the press asked Paul White on the White/Black name change and his reply was: "Our Anglo Saxon names of Paul White and Peter Black seemed to have absolved us from our previous existence. We got our wives Erin and Margaret, to thank for that."

Another reporter more intrepid than the first then asked, "Mr. White, when will Winnipeg become the pyrohy and holubtsi capital of Canada?"

"As soon as the Canadian government frees the remaining 2000 Ukrainians in concentration camps and apologizes that the interment was unjust and cruel."

"But the Canadian government's position is that the interment is legitimate under Canadian law of war, and there is no case for financial compensation or an apology."

"Then we'll have to educate the public about a historical wound that rankles us and perhaps other minorities in the future."

"What do you mean?"

"Let's put it this way. First it was the Aboriginal Indians, then the Chinese."

Paul White then took a short pause and read out loud the Chinese Immigration Act of 1885 that placed a head tax on all Chinese immigrants coming to Canada, forcing them to pay a fifty dollar fee to enter the country. "In 1900, the fee was raised to one-hundred dollars (a substantial amount of money at the time). In 1903, the amount was raised to five hundred dollars, the equivalency of two years' wages, which was a small fortune to the Chinese immigrants as well as other Canadians at the time.

Later, another law was passed, declaring that only one Chinese could come to Canada for every fifty tons of the ship they were traveling on, for that one voyage that means that only ten immigrants could come to Canada on a ship weighing five hundred tons.

This act was eventually superseded in 1923 by the Chinese Immigration Act of 1923, which banned Chinese immigration entirely. And now Ukrainians that are persecuted. Who knows what minority group might be next."

When the reporter shrugged his shoulders Paul White answered his own question. "It will probably be the Japanese Canadians and then the Muslim Arabs."

And with that prediction Paul White was correct. During World War 11 the property of the Japanese Canadians – land, business and other assets, were confiscated by the Canadian government and proceeds used to pay for their internment. In 1945, the government extended the Order in Council to force the Japanese Canadians to return to Japan and lose their Canadian citizenship, or move to eastern Canada. Even though the war over, it was illegal for Japanese Canadians to return to the Vancouver area until 1949.

Canada faced with growing pains had a challenge as it began to expand its future railway system and wait for another wave of Europeans to arrive in Western Canada where they wanted to live in.
And they came by the thousands.

Made in the USA
Charleston, SC
27 July 2015